MW01526668

1,000,000 Books

are available to read at

Forgotten Books

---◆---

www.ForgottenBooks.com

---◆---

Read online
Download PDF
Purchase in print

ISBN 978-1-333-59232-5
PIBN 10523837

This book is a reproduction of an important historical work. Forgotten Books uses
state-of-the-art technology to digitally reconstruct the work, preserving the original format
whilst repairing imperfections present in the aged copy. In rare cases, an imperfection in
the original, such as a blemish or missing page, may be replicated in our edition. We do,
however, repair the vast majority of imperfections successfully; any imperfections that
remain are intentionally left to preserve the state of such historical works.

Forgotten Books is a registered trademark of FB &c Ltd.
Copyright © 2018 FB &c Ltd.
FB &c Ltd, Dalton House, 60 Windsor Avenue, London, SW19 2RR.
Company number 08720141. Registered in England and Wales.

For support please visit www.forgottenbooks.com

1 MONTH OF
FREE
READING

at

www.ForgottenBooks.com

By purchasing this book you are eligible for one month membership to ForgottenBooks.com, giving you unlimited access to our entire collection of over 1,000,000 titles via our web site and mobile apps.

To claim your free month visit:

www.forgottenbooks.com/free523837

* Offer is valid for 45 days from date of purchase. Terms and conditions apply.

English
Français
Deutsche
Italiano
Español
Português

www.forgottenbooks.com

Mythology Photography **Fiction**
Fishing Christianity **Art** Cooking
Essays Buddhism Freemasonry
Medicine **Biology** Music **Ancient
Egypt** Evolution Carpentry Physics
Dance Geology **Mathematics** Fitness
Shakespeare **Folklore** Yoga Marketing
Confidence Immortality Biographies
Poetry **Psychology** Witchcraft
Electronics Chemistry History **Law**
Accounting **Philosophy** Anthropology
Alchemy Drama Quantum Mechanics
Atheism Sexual Health **Ancient History**
Entrepreneurship Languages Sport
Paleontology Needlework Islam
Metaphysics Investment Archaeology
Parenting Statistics Criminology
Motivational

THE
KAPPA SIGMA BOOK

A MANUAL

OF DESCRIPTIVE, HISTORICAL, AND STATISTICAL
FACTS CONCERNING
THE KAPPA SIGMA FRATERNITY

BY

BOUTWELL DUNLAP
National Historian of Kappa Sigma

PUBLISHED BY THE FRATERNITY

LIBRARY
OF THE
UNIVERSITY
OF
CALIFORNIA

NASHVILLE
THE CUMBERLAND PRESS
1907

K 8.

CONTENTS

INDEX OF ILLUSTRATIONS

PORTRAITS.

KAPPA SIGMA CHAPTER HOUSES.

OTHER ILLUSTRATIONS AND MAPS.

"A good fraternity is recognized as a good thing. Those who have enjoyed its fellowship understand its advantages. In those who have not experienced that blessing of boyhood life, no amount of argument can excite an appreciation of its value. The closest friendships you and I have to-day were formed before we became of age, in the walls of our chapter house. Age, occupation, distance, separation, new associations, have no influence upon friendships that are formed under such circumstances. You may not have seen him for a third of a century; you may not have heard his name for a generation; the path of his life may have led him to the Antipodes, but, when you come face to face with a boy who was initiated with you on a frosty autumn night, perhaps with absurd and silly ceremonies, the flame that often burns low, but can never be extinguished, will blaze up with a glow that will warm the lives of both of you; and you feel toward each other a sentiment that you have never felt toward any man since the day you graduated. I have met members of my fraternity in odd corners of the world. Among the Taoist temples in China; in the mines of the Andes; on the banks of the Nile, and although we were strangers before and have been strangers since, there was at least a few moments of gratification that encounters with other people could not have inspired. . . . There have been and always will be, abuses of the opportunities I have described, but those who are familiar with the history of college fraternities and will take the trouble to examine their catalogues will find that the high character of the men who have been members are the best endorsement of their advantages. By their personnel the Greek Letter Fraternities may justly be judged."—*William Eleroy Curtis.*

BOLOGNA

THE FOUNDING OF KAPPA SIGMA

One of the American universities of which our country should be most proud has recently celebrated with rejoicing the beginning of an era in her affairs, in the inauguration of her first president. New occasions now teach her new duties, larger opportunity leads her to take up tasks unthought-of even by her great first founder, but by virtue of her unique history, her matchless situation, her spirit of truth and honor, and most of all by the example of consecration to a worthy cause which those men afford who have served her so long and so faithfully for so small a material reward, she remains a blessing and a hope to all the region which receives good influences from her benign hand. She will continue to influence all that great civilization which has flowed in a stream from Virginia across the South and West, as Harvard and Yale have influenced that civilization which has gone out from New England to the Northwest, and met the other upon the Pacific coast.

The history of such an institution, even the history of its beginning, is not a mere matter of an act of legislature, or of the transfer of some millions from one account to another and the commissioning of an architect to make a new mixture of the old and the new. For the history of the University of Virginia there would be scant room in a manual of this size. Amid circumstances as romantic as ever surrounded the birth of any such order, Kappa Sigma came into existence; the only college fraternity of general extent to which the University of Virginia stands *in loco parentis*. There could be no nobler mother among the universities; and it is not those Kappa Sigmas alone who have stood beneath the Rotunda and lived on Lawns and Ranges, who feel pride and satisfaction at the influence, progress and prosperity of Old Virginia.

When, in 1868, William Grigsby McCormick, of Chicago and Baltimore, entered the University of Virginia, he found there a college system and a college life which could have been at no time paralleled anywhere in the North, nor, in all respects, even in the South. Many of the students were men in years, and every one was such in spirit and in mental development. Many had seen the face of war. The most punctilious rites of gentlemanly intercourse, between student and student and between students and faculty, were observed, and insisted upon by an inflexible sentiment. The system of the university's government left much to the choice of the individual student, asking only that his conduct should be regulated by a keen sense of honor, as the chivalrous and convivial South interpreted that word. In some sections of the country, many of the students would have been classed as roaring young blades; in other sections they might not have received so indulgent a title. Much went on that would have caused Cambridge to put up its shutters or New Haven to bar its doors. Yet that there was true metal under all the polish, manly integrity under all the youthful exuberance, not the South alone makes answer; for wherever there is a Virginia man from these buoyant years, there is an honored citizen whose worth compels his fellows' confidence.

The association of McCormick with Frank Courtney Nicodemus and Edmund Law Rogers had begun in Baltimore, the home of all three and the birthplace of the latter two. When the circle of friendship which enclosed these three was found, almost without their knowledge and wholly without their premeditation, to have included two others, George Miles Arnold and John Covert Boyd, within itself, the Fraternity had its new birth. The adoption of its historical and traditional name and ritualistic basis was a matter only of detail; its oath was merely the putting in words of vows already realized in the lives of the founders; its future extension was yet upon the knees of the gods. Adopting to some extent a form suggested by the customs of the student life in which they had a part, the Five Friends and Brothers organized the Kappa Sigma Fraternity.

THE ROTUNDA AND THE LAWNS, UNIVERSITY OF VIRGINIA

From the classic Rotunda which forms the center of Virginia's noble group of buildings, four colonnades, broken at intervals by taller structures, and modeled in every detail after the most authentic works of Grecian skill, stretch toward the south. As severely simple within as they were severely classic without, the rooms intended for the use of students had one attractive feature —the great fireplace, for the filling of which there was as yet no lack of oaken logs. In every chimney-corner a sheaf of long clay pipes betokened and invited brotherly intercourse. During his first year at the University, William Grigsby McCormick had

EAST LAWN AND ROTUNDA, UNIVERSITY OF VIRGINIA
Showing location of 46 East Lawn.   Present residence
of Prof. Wm. Minor Lile, of Zeta, at the right.

occupied a room (the front lower room of cottage C) in Dawson's Row, a group of dormitories just outside the main plan of the University buildings. In 1869 he occupied the room at 46 East Lawn, the situation of which, its present exterior and interior, is shown in the accompanying illustrations. The taller structure at the immediate right of 46 East Lawn in the view given is now, by the way, the residence of a Kappa Sigma, William Minor Lile, the dean of the law school of the University. Samuel Isham North and George Miles Arnold occupied this room in 1870-71. It was here that the first Constitution and Ritual of Kappa Sigma, a document which lies before the writer of these lines, was committed to writing.

The Founders were scattered about the university, so far as their "legal residences" were concerned. Nicodemus was at 6 West Range; Boyd and Rogers, as well as John E. Semmes, who was the first one added to the brotherhood after the original five, lived in "Social Hall," a small dormitory between the University proper and the town of Charlottesville. This house was so packed

EXTERIOR OF 46 EAST LAWN, UNIVERSITY OF VIRGINIA
Here Kappa Sigma in America was Founded

with men of promise that their names are worth mentioning. On the lower floor, besides Boyd and Semmes, were Chas. R. Hemphill, now a noted Presbyterian divine of Louisville; the cultivated and literary John Adger Clark, of South Carolina, now deceased; J. A. Crawford, now well known at the bar of Columbia, S. C.; and Robert B. Boylston, now a lawyer of Fairfield, S. C. Upstairs, Edmund Law Rogers occupied a room, and others on the same floor were John N. Steele, now an eminent

2

Baltimore lawyer and a partner of John E. Semmes, and his brother, I. Nevitt Steele, now of Trinity Church, New York. George Miles Arnold had a room on East Range; and when, early in 1870, he met Samuel Isham North upon the latter's arrival at the University from his Texas home, a great friendship sprang suddenly into immortal life. "The loveliest character I ever met," is North's judgment upon his friend and brother, after all the years. The reception of North into the new brotherhood

INTERIOR OF 46 EAST LAWN, UNIVERSITY OF VIRGINIA

followed almost as a matter of course. The members were always together. Such intimacies as existed within their number, like that between Arnold and North, were not allowed to disturb the general feeling of perfect fellowship. Formal meetings there seem to have been none. "Good fellows, good company, good manners, good morals and bright minds, full of spirits and all in for a good time," is Founder McCormick's description of them after a quarter of a century. Arnold was a leading spirit in the proceedings of the Fraternity, and at the suppers at "Brown's"

and "Ambroselli's," which were frequent occurrences. These fes-
tive gatherings were from the first a distinguishing feature of
the new Fraternity, and those Kappa Sigmas—and their name
is legion—who are *bons vivants* and whose wit flows most freely
around the festal board, may be assured that these characteristics
stamp them the true descendants of their forefathers in the Order, of whom, by the way, there was but one who ever took too
much wine, and not one who gave his strength to that which de-
stroyeth kings.   Edmund Law Rogers is remembered as one
whose light always shone brightly at these impromptu affairs, and
the rest were not behindhand.   If the record of these proceedings
but existed, some chapters might be added to the "Noctes Am-
brosianæ."

The question of a badge was very early taken up by the newly-
formed Fraternity, and after much discussion, the design due to
Edmund Law Rogers was adopted.   It is in every detail the same
as the present badge, save that the original examples were not
so markedly convex as those now made, and had a field of white
enamel in the center of the star instead of the present black.
The original constitution includes the full description of the
badge and the signification of its various parts and of the emblems borne upon it.   At the Christmas holidays of 1869, an
order for badges was placed with the Baltimore firm of Sadtler
& Sons, who had the work executed in New York.   After the
holidays, the Star and Crescent of Kappa Sigma was seen at
Virginia for the first time.   Badges of this early make still
exist, in the possession of George Leiper Thomas, Samuel
Isham North, Mrs. William Clark Whitford, and possibly others,
and one is seen on another page in the portrait of Samuel Isham North.   They were one inch in diameter, and were
originally furnished with a guard-chain and a chapter-pin of the
letter Zeta.   The chapter-pin has of late years been generally
abandoned, and the extreme size now allowable for the badge
is three-quarters of an inch.

The end of the college year '69-'70 put an end, for a time, to
the close associations of the original Five, who by this time had
united with themselves Semmes and North, as above stated.   In
the fall of 1870, Nicodemus was engaged in active business,

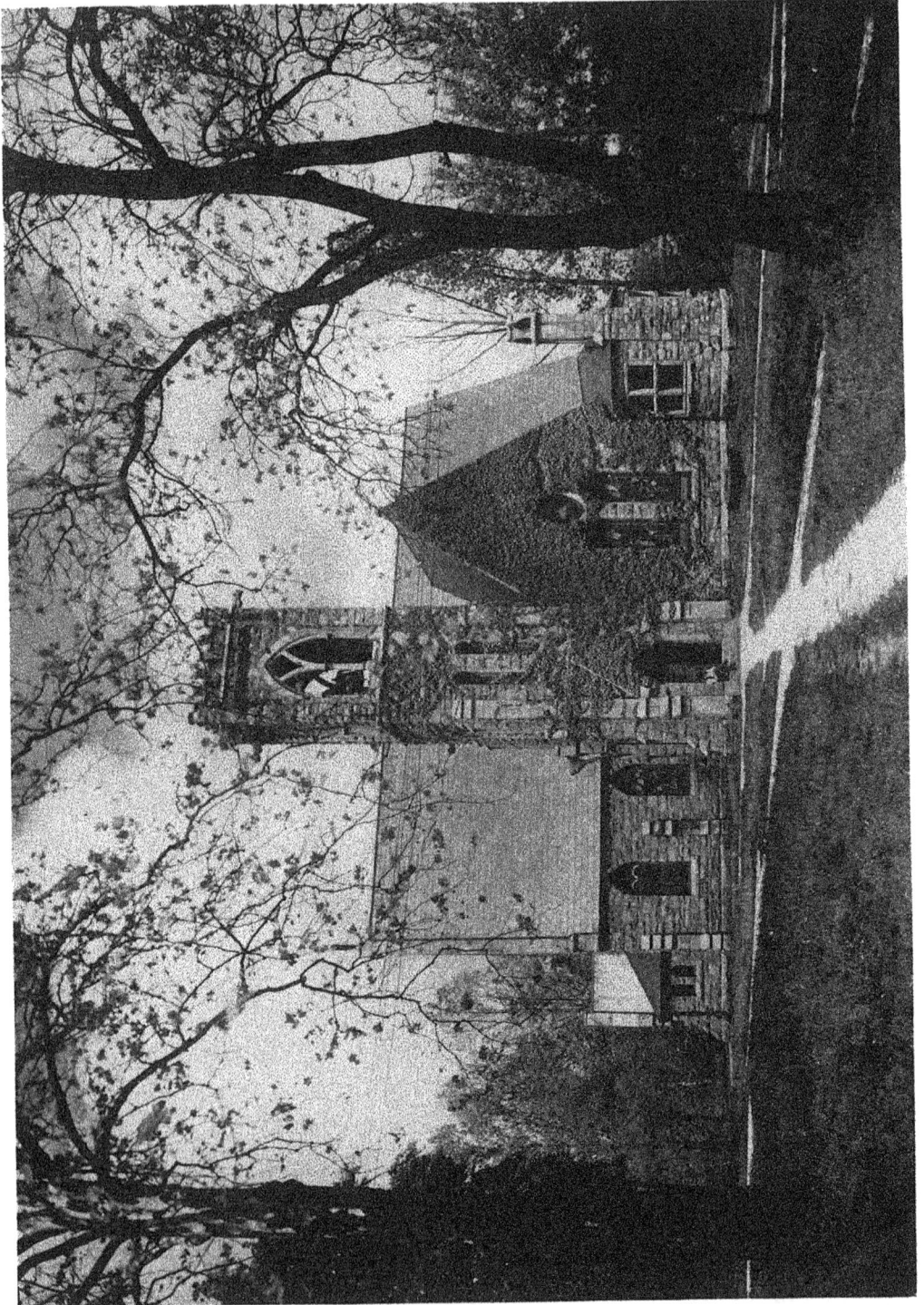

and decided not to pursue his university work further, while Mc-
Cormick has recorded the confession that he was very much in
love with the present Mrs. McCormick and was unwilling to separate himself from her immediate neighborhood by the distance
intervening between Baltimore and Charlottesville. Semmes not
returning until 1872, only Arnold, Boyd, Rogers and North were
found ready to carry on the work of the Fraternity when the
University reopened. All of these were interested in the Fraternity, which was just at its beginning, and willing to work for
it. So far as can be determined from the recollections of those
who survive, it was Arnold who had the rosiest dreams of the
future, dreams which have more than come true. With his as-
sociates, he laid the plans for the first extension of the Fraternity,
even assigning in advance the letters by which certain Chapters
should be designated; he fixed many matters which had been left
uncertain in the free and informal life of the previous year; and
he introduced the ritualistic work which, without any change
except certain amplifications of which the history is well known
to Kappa Sigmas, still awes and impresses the initiate when
rightly performed, and is pronounced by those in a position to
judge a most beautiful, consistent and fitting production. The
association of Samuel Isham North in this work with three of
the original Five of the preceding year gives him full and un-
questioned right to the honorable title of Founder. The work
of 1869 alone could not have led to the present development
of the Fraternity without the work of 1870; the work of 1870
undoubtedly had as its basis the work of 1869.

Much of the history of this important year is contained in the
oldest existing Kappa Sigma minutes, of which the original is in
the possession of the W. G. S., being held in trust by that official
for Zeta Chapter. As the minutes contain nothing in itself secret,
and as they introduce some other matters which must be presented, they are here given in full:

University of Virginia,
Nov. 7th, 1870.

The K. S. Society met at half past ten, at No. 46 East Lawn. After the
reading of the minutes of the last meeting the Society proceeded to business

ARNOLD AND NORTH
From a Tintype, 1870

and Mr. George L. Thomas whose name had been previously proposed, was then duly initiated as a member of the K. S. Society. Mr. Rogers made a motion that the following gentlemen, Viz Messrs. Toadvin, Walker and Hill be spoken to, and that they be invited to join our Society. Mr. Hill's name was subsequently withdrawn information having been rec'd that he had already become a member of the Delta Psi Society.

Mr. North was requested to speak to Mr. Walker.

Mr. Rogers "   "   "   "   "   " Toadvin.

There being no further business before the House, the Society adjourned, and to meet again at the discretion of the W. G. M., G. M. Arnold.

John C. Boyd, Secretary.

University of Virginia,
Dec. 2nd, 1870.

The K. S. Society met at the usual hour and all of the members being present they proceeded immediately to business. Mr. Rogers made motion that Mr. Toadvin be admitted into our society, which was unanimously adopted & Mr. Rogers was requested to invite him. After a good deal of fruitless debate as to the propriety of admitting more than one member at a meeting the Society adjourned.

J. C. Boyd,
Sec.

Edward S. Toadvin was duly initiated a member of the K. S. Fraternity on Dec. 12th 1870.

University of Virginia.
Feb. 25th, 1871.

The Society met at 10 p.m. The Grand Master, Mr. Arnold being compelled to leave by unavoidable circumstances, an election was held to fill his vacancy, resulting in the election of E. L. Rogers, Jr. to the responsible position of W. G. M. The other officers held their respective positions.

J. C. Boyd,
Sec.

Virginia University.
Feb. 30th, [sic] 1871.

The Kappa Sigma met at usual hour. No business being before the Society they adjourned.

Jno. C. Boyd,
Sec.

University of Virginia, March 18th, 71.

The K. S. Society met at the usual hour the W. Grand Master, Mr. Rogers holding the chair. After the usual preliminaries and the reading of the minutes of the last meeting Mr. W. C. Bowen of Northampton, N. C. was duly initiated into our Society. Information was rec'd that

Mr. Arnold was desirous of establishing a Chapter in New York where-
upon Mr. Rogers was authorized to have a copy sent him. The G. M.
then ordered the Scribe to have it forwarded immediately. After a few
interesting and sensible remarks by the G. M. the Society adjourned.

J. C. Boyd, Secretary.

Virginia University.

March 29th, 1871.

The K. S. Met to lament the departure of their worthy clubmate &
brother Saml. I North—whose absence will be felt so deeply by all of us—
After taking business matters into consideration we sat down to a finely
prepared supper, where till late did we enjoy the fruits of Bacchus, at
2 o'clock the Society adjourned.

J. C. Boyd, Secretary.

University of Virginia.

April 30th 1871.

We very much regret to state that Brother J. C. Boyd has left the Uni
versity, as he was most highly esteemed by all the members of his Society.
Hoping that he may always prosper in his future career we bid him an
affectionate adieu.

E. L. Rogers, Jr.,
per Wm. Whitford
Secretary.

It was in this year that members of the Fraternity rented and
occupied a cottage, the property of the famous Latin professor,
Gildersleeve, which thereby became the first fraternity house of
Kappa Sigma, and apparently the first fraternity house in the
South. George Leiper Thomas and Edmund Law Rogers lived
in it. With them was Robert S. McCormick (the present Ambassador to France, and a brother of William Grigsby McCormick), who had been very intimate with the founders of the year
before but who himself became a member of Sigma Chi. Here
took place one act of the thrilling series of events known since in
the Fraternity as "The Defense of Miles Arnold," which served
to test the oaths of the new brotherhood and the feeling of mutual confidence among the students of the University.

To say that political and social conditions in the South were at
this time "unsettled" is to use as mild language as if one were to
call Paradise enjoyable or the lower regions temperately warm.

FIRST KAPPA SIGMA HOUSE, UNIVERSITY OF VIRGINIA, 1870-71

The negro was "on the front seat of the band-wagon," as a brother has put it; and the white citizen who confronted a colored man in any court had every presumption against him. The hot-blooded Southerners of the University went armed, and frequently indulged in nocturnal pistol-practice, by way of warning to all whom it might concern that they were prepared to take matters into their own hands whenever necessary. Miles Arnold was what those nourished on icicles are accustomed to call a fire-eater; though of no overbearing disposition he had the temper which went with his nicknames of "the Count" and "the little Spaniard," and he was never unarmed. On a bitter day in February, 1871, he had been several miles from Charlottesville, across the Rivanna river, to call on a young lady. When he was about to leave her home, she, after the hospitable fashion of the time, pressed him to fortify himself against the outer cold by a sufficient number of apple-jacks. On reaching Charlottesville Arnold seems to have taken further similar measures with the same intent. Finding his conduct gratuitously called in question by a son of Ham, he made no long argument of the matter, but fired upon his assailant and laid him low. It turned out that, owing to the well-known thickness of the African cranium, the wound was not mortal; but, in ignorance of this fact, and knowing that there was danger should a negro mob be formed, and almost equal danger should he fall into the hands of what in those times and in that region passed for law, Arnold at once sought his friend and brother North, in their room upon the University campus, and told him what had happened.

E. Stanley Toadvin, who had met Arnold as he came up, was at once dispatched toward the town, to put the sheriff and his posse, who were known to be approaching, on a false scent if possible. North spirited Arnold away to a room in another part of the campus, and sent out word to the other Kappa Sigmas and his Texan friends—many of whom, owing to the constant association of North and Arnold, believed the latter a Texan—to rally to his defense. Toadvin, returning, assumed the leadership of these, while the sheriff and posse searched in Arnold's and the neighboring rooms in vain. They then turned their attention, perhaps by the suggestion of some brother who knew where

Dr. Maupin (Chm. of Faculty)
Dr. McGuffey   Dr. Cabell
John B. Minor
Dr. Smith   Dr. Davis
Dr. Mallet   Dr. Harrison
Col. Peters   Prof. Gildersleeve
Dr. Chancellor   Dr. Holmes
Lib'n Westenbaker   Prof. de Vere
Prof. Boeck   Col. Venable   Dr. Southall
                                 Maj. Peyton (Proctor)

FACULTY, UNIVERSITY OF VIRGINIA, 1869-70
From contemporary photo. by Roads, Charlottesville

Arnold really was, to the Gildersleeve cottage, the Kappa Sigma house, where Arnold might be supposed to have gone.

George Leiper Thomas was sitting alone in the lower room of the cottage, nursing a crippled knee, when Robert McCormick rushed in upon him and dropped a loaded shotgun in his lap with the forcible injunction "Defend your fraternity brother." The situation was explained in a few words, and Thomas was arranged so as to form a battery of one piece commanding the front door and the approaches thereto. The door being opened, Mc-

McCORMICK OBSERVATORY UNIVERSITY OF VIRGINIA
The gift of L. J. McCormick, an uncle of the Founder

Cormick and Rogers took their positions outside as if to prevent any approach to the house from the rear, and, on the coming of the sheriff, parleyed with that officer at great length, finally convincing him that Arnold was not in the house.

Meanwhile, it had been reported to North that a mob of negroes was forming to search the University grounds for Arnold. "Some negroes saved their lives by not finding us that night," says Dr. North in reminiscences of the affair. North's horse, and a fresh one for Arnold, were brought to the most retired side of the campus, and forty armed Texans and Kappa Sigmas escorted Arnold to the spot. By this time it had been dark for some hours. Arnold, with North as his escort, rode fifteen miles into the country, to the house of the grandfather of Arnold's sweetheart whose well-meant prescription of apple-jack had been the beginning of all the trouble. The two riders missed the ford of the Rivanna, and were nearly ready to perish with cold when, about two the next morning, they reached a friendly shelter. Arnold went on to friends in another county the next day, and, after some weeks, went to New York to enter a medical college there, where his inseparable friend North soon joined him. Arnold's resignation as a student was accepted by the Virginia faculty without prejudice; the Ethiopian sufferer soon recovered; and thus by the quick wit of Kappa Sigmas what might have been a mournful tragedy was turned into a drama to be a stirring memory of years afterward, and a lesson of the strength of a fraternal obligation.

A month after the departure of North, that of Boyd is recorded. The work of the Chapter, as it may now be called, appears to have ended for the year with the loss of three of the Founders in succession.

The rest belongs to the early history of the Fraternity and of Zeta Chapter. Let that which is here set down suffice to show that American Kappa Sigma sprang from no rivalry, discontent or disappointment, but solely from the free spirit of brotherhood in loyal hearts. Already plans are being considered to celebrate, in 1919, the fiftieth anniversary of the founding and to make the event unparalleled among such fêtes.

WILLIAM GRIGSBY McCORMICK
1905

THE FOUNDERS OF KAPPA SIGMA

It is said that Boston asks concerning a stranger, "What does he know?" New York, "How much is he worth?" Philadelphia, "Who was his grandfather?" and Washington, "What can he do?" The founders of Kappa Sigma could pass this whole examination with credit. The too early death of two of the original Five Friends and Brothers cut short lives in which the spirit of a noble ancestry was fully shown; the founders who survive are honored citizens whose worthy achievements in widely various walks of life exemplify the catholic scope of the Fraternity which they founded. The true romance of the Founding having been told in the preceding chapter, as fully as it can ever be given to the general public, it remains to show who the Founders were and to tell the story of their later lives.

WILLIAM GRIGSBY McCORMICK

A volume of four hundred seventy-eight pages (Ancestral Record and Biography of the McCormick Family: By Leander James McCormick. Chicago, 1896) is required to display the ramifications, in Pennsylvania, Kentucky and Virginia, of this fine old Irish Presbyterian family, of the self-same breed as their fellow-countymen who, settling in Augusta county, Virginia, gave America scores of her generals and statesmen. It is possible to mention here only that branch of the McCormicks, celebrated in our national annals for a hundred years, from which our founder comes; a line known not alone for its enormous wealth, but also for the genius displayed by it in other fields than those of mere money making, and for its alliances with people distinguished otherwise than by their material possessions; and among the families of American multimillionaires, the only one which traces its origin to the South.

The first of the name to become world-famous was Robert McCormick (1780-1846), the inventor, who laid the foundation of the family fortunes. He lived at "Walnut Grove," Augusta county, Virginia, an estate of two thousand acres into which he came by inheritance. Among his eight sons and daughters were Cyrus H. McCormick, the Chicago inventor and financier, whose daughter married Emmons Blaine (son of James G. Blaine),

WILLIAM
GRIGSBY
McCORMICK
1869

and whose son married Edith Rockefeller (daughter of John D. Rockefeller); Leander J. McCormick, who gave the McCormick observatory to the University of Virginia; and William Sanderson McCormick, allied with his brothers in the perfecting of the great inventions which influenced the agricultural development of a world. William S. McCormick married Mary Ann Grigsby, daughter of Col. Reuben Grigsby, of "Hickory Hill," Rockbridge county, Virginia, and cousin of Hugh Blair Grigsby, a celebrated president of William and Mary College. Of this union, the second born was William Grigsby McCormick, Founder of Kappa Sigma, whose elder brother, Robert S. McCormick, late Ambassador to France, married a daughter of Joseph Medill, the man who made the Chicago *Tribune*. A son of Robert S. McCormick married Senator Hanna's daughter Ruth; three sisters of the Founder married into well-known Chicago families; and the important alliances formed by various members of the third and fourth generations are too numerous to be mentioned here.

William Grigsby McCormick was born June 3, 1851, in the McCormick home in Chicago, on Cass and Illinois streets. After receiving his primary education in private schools of the city, he was a student in the preparatory department of the old University of Chicago. His mother, widowed in 1865, soon afterward removed to Baltimore, from which city young McCormick went in October, 1868, to the University of Virginia, returning to that University in 1869. There the associations, already begun in the case of some of the founders, developed, as we have seen, into the Fraternity.

Leaving the University of Virginia in May, 1870, he spent six months in foreign travel, accompanied by his brother Robert and by a cousin. England, Ireland, Scotland and the Continent were visited. Returning to Baltimore in November of the same year, young McCormick followed his natural bent by associating himself with the banking house of John S. Gittings & Co., in whose employ he remained for two years. His happy marriage to Eleanor Brooks, daughter of Walter Booth Brooks (president of the Canton Company and son of a former president of the B. & O.) was the next important event of his life. At this first Kappa Sigma wedding, which occurred October 23, 1873, at the Brown Memorial Church of Baltimore, George Leiper Thomas was a groomsman and Edmund Law Rogers a guest. Returning late in 1874 from a year of foreign travel, Mr. and Mrs. McCormick spent a few months in Baltimore, removing in February, 1875, to Chicago.

Brother McCormick now entered upon the active business career which continued until his retirement in 1900. As a member of the firm of McCormick Bros. & Findlay, and later of W. G. McCormick & Co., with offices in Chicago and New York, he was

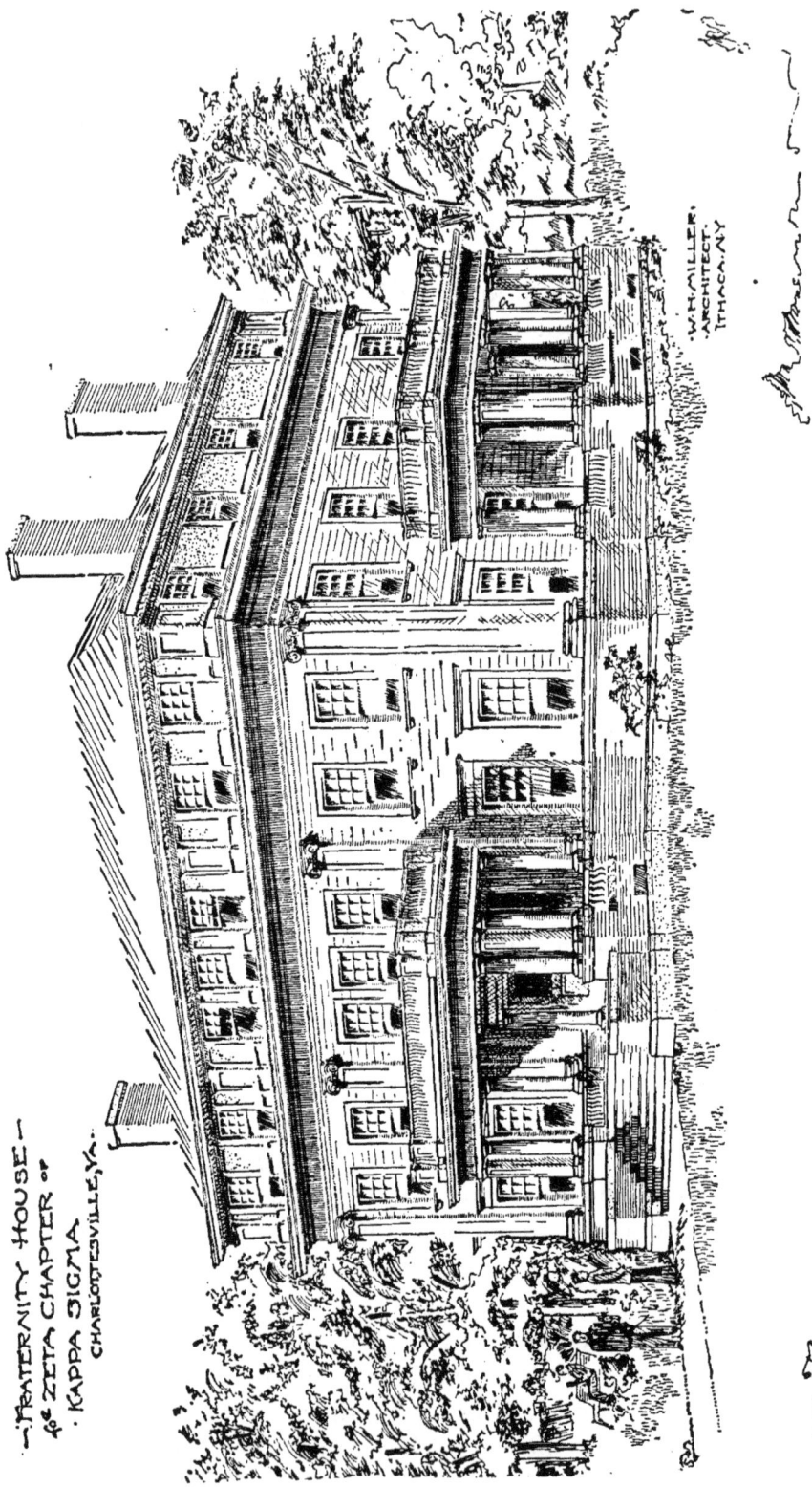

FRATERNITY HOUSE
for ZETA CHAPTER of
KAPPA SIGMA
CHARLOTTESVILLE, VA.

W.H.MILLER
ARCHITECT
ITHACA, N.Y.

McCORMICK HALL, PROPOSED KAPPA SIGMA HOUSE, VIRGINIA

engaged in the fire insurance and real estate business until 1884. In that year he became a member of the Chicago board of trade and of the grain and stock brokerage firm of Smith, McCormick & Co. In the following year, W. G. McCormick became a member of the New York stock exchange; and after some changes of business relationships, the firm of W. G. McCormick & Co., having its offices in New York, Chicago and St. Louis, was organized. In 1891 Brother McCormick transferred his business interests to the well-known Schwartz-Dupee combination, with which he was associated until 1893. After a brief retirement from business, he reentered the arena in 1894 as a partner in the widely-known and successful firm of Price, McCormick & Co., which firm was terminated in 1900. Brother McCormick's only active entrance into politics was in 1880, when, against his expressed wish, friends placed him on the Democratic ticket for alderman from the eighteenth ward of the city of Chicago, a ward which had not elected a Democrat for more than twenty years. Brother McCormick was elected, to the surprise of many political wiseacres of the city.

He is well-known in the principal cities of the world, and has many friends in both hemispheres. He is a member of no secret order except the Kappa Sigma Fraternity. He is or has been a member of the Chicago, Union, Athletic and Washington Park clubs of Chicago, the Union, Manhattan and Whist clubs of New York, the Pickwick club of New Orleans, the Alston and Maryland clubs of Baltimore, and the Kennel club of Baltimore county, Maryland. The pictures of Brother McCormick accompanying this volume are the only ones he has ever given out for publication anywhere.

Seven children, of whom six are living, have been born to Mr. and Mrs. McCormick. One of the four daughters married Herbert S. Stone, the Chicago publisher, son of Melville E. Stone, manager of the Associated Press. A son, Walter Brooks McCormick, is vice-president and general manager of the McCormick Coal Company, of Kansas, one of his father's enterprises; the other son, Chauncey Brooks McCormick, is a Yale '07 man and a member of Alpha Delta Phi. Since the retirement of Brother

McCormick from active business life in 1900, the family home has been at their country house in Goshen, Virginia, and at the Brooks mansion, "Clover Dale," Baltimore.

GEORGE MILES ARNOLD

The father of George Miles Arnold was George Anson Arnold, a native of Troy, N. Y., and son of Dr. George Arnold, of Newport, R. I., who came of a family well-known in that section. George Anson Arnold married Mary Antoinette Filkins, cele-

GEORGE
MILES
ARNOLD
1871

brated beauty of Troy, and engaged in a wholesale business in Mobile, Ala., where he prospered. On one of the Arnolds' yearly visits to Troy, George Miles Arnold was born, August 27, 1851.

After receiving his first training at the Union Hill boarding school, Monroe county, N. Y., and at Dr. Davis' academy for boys, Bloomfield, N. J., Arnold entered the academic department of the University of Virginia in 1869, his chief studies being Latin, French and mathematics. Small but well built, speaking French, Spanish and Italian fluently, he was a typical young Southerner of those stirring times. Although carrying no Spanish blood, nevertheless, on account of his proficient knowledge of the language, he was known to his friends and

CALIFORN

admirers as "the little Spaniard." From students of Kappa Sigma history he has later received the title of "the first S. A. Jackson." All the surviving founders agree in praise of his devotion from the first to the cause of the Fraternity. "He gave nearly his whole time to the society," says one. In the summer of 1870, he began, with Samuel Isham North, his nearest and dearest friend even within Kappa Sigma, a course in medicine at the University, under Harrison, the famous and beloved professor.

GEORGE
MILES
ARNOLD
About 1870

In February, 1871, the occurrence elsewhere related made it necessary for his friends and brothers to protect him from the consequences of a rash and hasty act, and caused his withdrawal from the University—the authorities, after investigation, accepting his resignation as a student and dismissing him with a clear record.

He shortly entered the medical college of New York University, and by the end of the scholastic year 1872, had completed the medical course according to the requirements of the time. Being still under age, his degree was not conferred upon him until the following year, 1873. He studied at Bellevue Hospital medical college in 1872-'73, and received a diploma also from this institution. He also served for a time as resident physician at the E. and P. Hospital, Bedford Island, and in 1873 began to practice. Later he was resident physician at the Convalescent Hospital, Hart's Island, and, having become a Master Mason of Lebanon lodge in 1873, was in 1874-'75 vice-president and examining physician of the Washington Masonic Mutual Benefit Association, of New York.

Founder Arnold's marriage occurred on September 8, 1874,

GEORGE
MILES
ARNOLD
1876

at the Jane St. M. E. church, New York, the officiating minister being the Rev. Dr. Hamlin. The bride was Miss Minnie J. Law, daughter of Robert J. Law, a wealthy real estate owner of the city, a Mason, and a veteran of the Civil War, being one of the first to go out with the New York Seventh. For a number of years the Arnolds resided at 105 east 71st St., New York, and their home was a meeting-place for Kappa Sigmas of that early day. The Star and Crescent, illuminated in the size of the early badges, appeared on Arnold's note-paper; he spoke much of the Fraternity, corresponding with his friends North and Boyd continually, and often entertaining as his guests S. A. Jackson and Ed. Law Rogers, Jr., the latter of whom claimed kinship with

Mrs. Arnold through their common descent from the Maryland Laws.

Dr. and Mrs. Arnold were for years regular attendants upon St. James' Episcopal church, New York, and here for five years, until the demands of a constantly increasing practice obliged him to abandon it, Arnold had a Bible class of young men, who were closely drawn to him by his ever attractive personality.

To Dr. Arnold and his wife there were born eight children. Of the sad death of five of these, the widowed mother speaks seldom and with reluctance. Three died within one period of six weeks; after an interval of five years, death claimed two in one day: and all were carried off by the same disease, diphtheria, which Dr. Arnold was accustomed to meet and to vanquish in his practice, having never lost a case. A lover of his home and family, the effect of these losses never left him. He threw himself more and more earnestly into his active work, becoming regardless of his own health; and on January 25, 1890, pneumonia due to exposure resulted in his death, after an illness of but a few days. His body reposes in Woodlawn Cemetery. Mrs. Arnold, with her three living children, two daughters and a son, found a home with her mother for five years, until that lady's death, and then removed to her present residence, 57 W. 124th St., New York. One daughter is attending the New York Normal College, and the son, Robert Miles Arnold, aged now eighteen, is a student of C. C. N. Y.

Other Kappa Sigmas have been better known than Miles Arnold, but none has ever been better loved. Peace to his ashes! The Fraternity would have delighted in these latter days to honor him living; dead, it reveres his memory.

EDMUND LAW ROGERS

The third of the original Five, and the designer of the badge of Kappa Sigma, was the son of Edmund Law Rogers, Sr., and Charlotte (Plater) Rogers, and was born in Baltimore, July 1, 1850. He was descended through his paternal grandmother from Mrs. Martha Custis, afterwards the wife of George Washington; whose son, John Parke Custis, early wedded pretty Eleanor

Calvert, daughter of Benedict Calvert, a head of the old-time Maryland family. Their daughter, Eliza Custis, married Thomas Law, whose brother, the first Baron Ellenborough, was leading counsel for Warren Hastings before the House of Lords in 1788, and Lord Chief Justice of England from 1802 to 1818. . Thomas Law was of no less worth. Before coming to America, he had been governor of a province in India, under Cornwallis as governor-general, in 1786 and later. His devotion to his adopted country was shown when, in 1814, after the burning of the

EDMUND
LAW
ROGERS
About 1883

national capitol by the British, he with another purchased a house in Washington and allowed Congress the use of it as a capitol building until better quarters could be erected—by this one act preventing the removal of the capital of the nation from Washington. Eliza Law, daughter of Thomas Law, married Lloyd Nicholas Rogers, of Baltimore, and their son was General Edmund Law Rogers, Sr., father of our founder.

The Rogers line was also one of distinction. Nicholas Rogers, father of Lloyd Nicholas Rogers, was a student in Scotland at the time when the Revolution began. Hurrying back to his country by way of France, to give himself to the cause of freedom, he became an aide-de-camp to General de Coudray, and was afterward Baron de Kalb's adjutant during the dreadful winter at Valley Forge. Soon after the close of the Revolution, Colonel Rogers married Eleanor Buchanan, daughter of Lloyd Buchanan and granddaughter of one of the founders of Baltimore. With her there came into the Rogers family the country-seat of five hundred and fifty acres, then known as "Auchentoroly," which

EDMUND
LAW
ROGERS
In character

the city of Baltimore bought from Lloyd Nicholas Rogers in 1859 for $550,000, and which has now become Druid Hill, one of the surpassingly beautiful and perfect parks of the world. Gen. Edmund Law Rogers, Sr., who died about 1895, was a prominent and wealthy citizen of Baltimore, and held many positions of honor and trust in the city and state. His wife, Charlotte Plater, was a descendant of George Plater, one of the colonial governors of Maryland and a member of the Council. Their only surviving child is Charlotte, wife of Professor Kirby Flower Smith, of Johns Hopkins.

Edmund Law Rogers, Jr., was prepared for the University at the well-known academy of James Kinnier, in Baltimore, where Founder F. C. Nicodemus was among his classmates. Entering the University of Virginia in 1869, he was graduated in an academic course. He then took up the study of architecture. Thoroughly artistic in his temperament, none who knew him doubt that had he been under the kindly spur of necessity he might have achieved eminence in his profession, and, given the ordinary span of life, have been one of our country's chief apostles of a noble art which is just now coming to its own among us. Private theatricals had given him a liking for the stage. It amused him to act, and, free from personal anxieties and cares, he enjoyed the life behind the footlights. Handsome and clever, he was always in demand for leading parts and in the support of popular stars, from 1880, when he entered upon his stage career, to the time of his death. At one time he played in "stock" with Ada Rehan, and later he had the part, which one of his few extant pictures shows to have been easily assumed by him, of a Southern planter in Boucicault's drama of "The Octoroon." Upon the stage he was known as Leslie Edmunds. Kindly, polished, full of quiet humor, a citizen of the world who loved the world in which he dwelt, his old friends found much pleasure in their continued association with him while he lived. He was a member of the Lambs club, of New York, and of the old Alston club of Baltimore. He married Miss Anna Carleton, of Boston, who survived him but a few years. His death occurred in New York, December 19, 1893; he was buried, from the old Rogers residence in Baltimore, in the Buchanan and Rogers burying-ground in Druid Hill, reserved to the family use perpetually when the sale to the city was made. Among the pall-bearers was George Leiper Thomas, his early brother in the parent Chapter of Kappa Sigma.

FRANK COURTNEY NICODEMUS

Frank Courtney Nicodemus is one of the five surviving children of Josiah Courtney Nicodemus and Mary Jane (Montandon) Nicodemus, both from old American and Maryland families; and is a native, and a life-long resident, of Baltimore. One of his sisters is the wife of Edwin Warfield, "the first gentleman of the South," the present Governor of Maryland. Before entering the University of Virginia, young Nicodemus was a student at Kinnier's Academy in his native city, where he was associated with Edmund Law Rogers, Jr. Leaving the University in the spring of 1870, he was taken into the office of his father's firm, Smith & Nicodemus. In 1874 he became a partner in the same firm, and in the following year he formed a partnership with his

FRANK
COURTNEY
NICODEMUS
1904

father, under the title of J. C. Nicodemus & Son. The new firm engaged in a general investment and brokerage business for the following four years. In 1879, Brother Nicodemus formed the firm of F. C. Nicodemus & Co., for the manufacture of boilers, engines and machinery; withdrawing from this firm in 1885, he became treasurer of the Baltimore postoffice. In March, 1891, he was offered the general agency for Maryland of the Connecticut Mutual Life Insurance Company, which he continues to hold.

Brother Nicodemus has been a member of the old Alston club,

and of the Maryland club, of Baltimore. He has always had a part in the social life of his city, and has been intimately associated with some of the older and younger Kappa Sigmas there. He was married March 26, 1879, in the Franklin Street Presbyterian Church, Baltimore, to Mary Field Weeks, daughter of John L. Weeks, a member of the Baltimore firm of Woods, Weeks & Co. To Mr. and Mrs. Nicodemus were born four children: John Lee Nicodemus, who is about to become an officer in the regular army; Frank Courtney Nicodemus, Jr., a graduate of the law school of the University of Maryland and a bright young member of the firm of Pierce & Greer, of New York, one of the strongest law partnerships in the United States; Mary Nicodemus; and Gordon Kirkland Nicodemus, who has just entered upon business life. After the death of his first wife, Brother Nicodemus was again married, in 1891, to Miss Florence B. Smith, of Baltimore. At 1815 Park avenue, Baltimore, is the pleasant home of the family.

JOHN COVERT BOYD

John Covert Boyd, who has been connected with the Navy medical corps for more than thirty years, was born December 24, 1850, near Bradford Springs, Sumter county, South Carolina. His grandfather was Dr. John Boyd, physician and planter, and his father, William Simms Boyd, was a graduate of the South Carolina Medical College, though he devoted his attention to the management of his estate rather than to the practice of his profession. An ancestor in the paternal line was General Richard Richardson, 1704-1780, who attained to distinction in the colonial wars and in the Revolution. An account of his services and a history of his descendants is to be found in Johnson's "Traditions of the Revolution," and in Mrs. E. F. Ellet's "Women of the American Revolution," where the life of General Richardson's wife, who was Elizabeth Canty, of South Carolina, is given. John Covert Boyd's mother was Laura Nelson (Covert) Boyd, a daughter of John Covert, a minister of the Dutch Reformed Church and a graduate of Columbia and of Princeton Seminary. After being prepared for college in private schools of Charleston, S. C., John Covert Boyd spent two years at the University of Virginia, from 1869 to 1871, beginning the medical course in the second year. He then entered the medical department of the University of the City of New York, from which he received the degree of M.D. in 1872. After a year as interne in the Jersey City Charity Hospital, he was appointed an Assistant Surgeon in the Navy medical corps, and since that time has been continuously connected therewith, having risen through the grades of Passed Assistant Surgeon, Surgeon, and Medical Inspector, to

JOHN
COVERT
BOYD
1905

that of Medical Director. The detailed record of his career would fill several of these pages. He has seen service both afloat and ashore; was for eight years assistant to the chief of the naval Bureau of Medicine and Surgery; was detailed as a delegate to represent the medical department of the Navy at a meeting of th Association of Military Surgeons of the United States, held in Buffalo, in 1895; was again detailed as a delegate to the International Tuberculosis Congress, Berlin, 1899. Since 1902 he has been a professor in the Naval Medical College, Washington, in which institution he is second in seniority, and a member of the Board for examination and promotion of medical officers. Throughout his professional career he has been the author of numerous reports upon technical subjects, and he is at present engaged, under the supervision of the Surgeon-General of the Navy, in the preparation of a book of instructions for medical officers, which will make a volume of four hundred pages.

Dr. Boyd is a Fellow of the New York Academy of Medicine; a member of the Association of Military Surgeons of the United States and of the American Medical Association; an honorary member of the Medical Society of the District of Columbia; a member of the Philadelphia Academy of Natural Sciences and of the Archæological Institute of America. On January 16, 1905, President Roosevelt designated him as one of the incorporators of the American National Red Cross, and appointed him a member of the Central Committee of that body. On the meeting of the incorporators he was made a member of the Executive Committee of the Red Cross. His club membership includes the Metropolitan, Washington, the Reform, New York, and the New York Yacht Club. Attractive and magnetic, a typical Southerner and a loyal American, Dr. Boyd is known not only as the best informed man in the Navy, but also as the best loved man in it. It is said on good authority that he has to his credit the highest grade ever made in an examination for Passed Assistant Surgeon. He was married June 24, 1887, to Miss Katharine Dorr Willard, of Washington, a daughter of C. C. Willard, of the well-known Washington family, and a descendant of Simon Willard, once president of Harvard. With their son and daughter, Dr. and Mrs. Boyd occupy a delightful home at 1315 P Street, northwest, Washington.

JOHN E. SEMMES

John E. Semmes was born at Cumberland, Md., July 1, 1851. The Semmes family in America is a distinguished one, especially in the Navy, and is descended from Joseph Semmes, originally of Norman ancestry, who came to Maryland from England in 1688. Representatives of the family living in northern France offered their services to Admiral Semmes on board the *Alabama* at Cherbourg just before the engagement with the *Kearsarge*. The father of John E. Semmes was Samuel M. Semmes, of Mary-· land, a lawyer by profession. Receiving his early education under private tutors and in Chestnut Hill School, John E. Semmes entered the University of Virginia October 18, 1869. He was graduated upon the completion of a course in analytical chemis- try, and soon afterward entered the Navy as secretary to Com- modore John Guest, his maternal uncle. Later, he prepared for

JOHN
EDWARD
SEMMES
1905

the bar in the law school of the University of Maryland, and entered the office of the late John H. B. Latrobe. He is now a member of the law firm of Steele & Semmes, of Baltimore, is prominent at the bar of that city, and was at one time city solici- tor. One of his partners, John N. Steele, was with him at Virginia in 1869-70. Brother Semmes was married to Frances Hayward, daughter of Nehemiah P. Hayward, of New Hamp- shire, and Prudence (Carman) Hayward, a descendant of Cap- tain Robert North, prominent in the early history of Baltimore.

He is a member of the Maryland club and of the Bachelors' Cotillion club of Baltimore. In the early days of Kappa Sigma, he was an intimate associate of the lamented Rogers.

SAMUEL ISHAM NORTH

Samuel Isham North was born May 14, 1849, on his father's farm in De Witt county, Texas, and received his early education

SAMUEL
ISHAM
NORTH
1904

· in the schools of that state. Early in January, 1870, he entered the University of Virginia, forming that deep and lasting friendship with George Miles Arnold which led to North's early union with the just-formed Fraternity. The work of Rogers, Arnold and North, is known to those acquainted with the history of the secret work of the Fraternity, and has been spoken of in the preceding chapter, in so far as it may be told in these pages. After devoting some time to academic studies, North, with Arnold, entered upon the study of medicine, taking the first year of the regular medical course. Leaving Virginia in the spring of.

1871 to take the summer course at the University of New York, he passed his final examinations in September, 1871, at the latter institution, though on account of a regulation as to time of residence the degree was not conferred upon him until the following March. At that time, after a competitive examination, Dr. North won the position of interne at Roosevelt hospital, where he served eighteen months. He then became one of sixteen applicants for interne at the Woman's hospital, the examination for which is said to be one of the hardest in the country. North won the position. The illness of his father soon demanded his return to Texas, and in 1874 he began to practice in Galveston. Considerations of health necessitated a change of climate, and he removed to Cuero, in his native county, and in 1882 to Clayton, New Mexico, where he has since led the self-denying life of a busy doctor; the monotony of which he has varied by a successful venture in Hereford cattle. His fellow-citizens have also provided him with occupation for his rare moments of leisure by making him their county superintendent of schools.

On June 25, 1884, Dr. North married Eliza Gordon, daughter of Jonathan W. Gordon, a major of regulars and afterward a celebrated criminal lawyer of Indianapolis. Their son, Samuel Gordon North, born in 1885, is attending Washington and Lee University, and is an active member of Mu of Kappa Sigma. The four hundred Kappa Sigmas who attended the St. Louis Conclave remember the good gray doctor, and understand how much of the present beauty and strength of the Fraternity is due to the work performed by him, with the lamented Rogers and Arnold.

GEORGE LEIPER THOMAS

George Leiper Thomas, the first regular initiate the date of whose initiation is precisely known, was born in Baltimore, September 10, 1852. His father was John Henry Thomas, a member of the Baltimore bar for fifty-four years, a distinguished and able lawyer, and a graduate of Princeton. After attending private schools in Baltimore, George Thomas went to Europe in the summer of 1868, for a year of study and travel. After attending

lectures at Lausanne he went to Dresden, and was at the Circus
Renz on the night of July 19, 1870, when the performance was
brought to an abrupt end by the announcement, made from
the ring by Renz, the proprietor, of the declaration of war by
France upon Germany. Thomas then went to Berlin, where he
remained a spectator of events until the end of the Franco-
Prussian war. Returning to America, he entered the University
of Virginia in the fall of 1870, and was made a member of Kappa
Sigma at its first meeting of which the contemporary minute re-

GEORGE
LEIPER
THOMAS
1905

mains, November 7, 1870. He was one of those who lived in the
first Kappa Sigma house during the year '70-'71, and many par-
ticulars of the early history may be derived from his recollections
of the intimacy existing among the members, and of their habits
and customs. He was the intimate friend and associate of Edmund Law Rogers until the death of the latter, and has kept up
his acquaintance with other pioneer Kappa Sigmas. He received
the degree of LL.B. from the University of Maryland, in 1873,
and has practiced law in Baltimore ever since.

THE EUROPEAN TRADITION

The Fraternity is alone among the university societies of the country in a traditional and legendary European origin.

History gives us the information that there existed in European universities secret orders among students. About the year 1400, as is well known, there came to the oldest university in the world, Bologna, the Greek scholar Manuel Chrysoloras (1355?-1415) who gave to the world as his pupils many distinguished scholars. He was the author of *Erotemata Quaestiones,* one of the first Greek grammars used in Italy. He is traditionally asserted to have founded at the university a secret Order of students for mutual protection against Baltasare Cossa, at that time governor of the city, who practiced extortion upon the students, even sending out bands of his followers to rob them as they approached the university. The Order continued to exist, and spread first to the University of Florence, and then to the other three of the five great universities—Paris, Orleans and Montpelier. The lodges or circles among these scholars were known as Kohaths. They flourished throughout the revival of learning, enrolling the names of Bruni, Politian, the de Medicis, Michael Angelo, Chalcondylas, Bracciolini, and many others— poets, artists and wits. At one time it was intended to name all of the American chapters after these celebrities.

In modern times the Order became practically extinct, but its secrets and symbols are said to have been preserved by a few noble families of Italy and France—principally in the de Bardi family. Its ritual, not a sophomore document, and peculiarly appropriate to a university society, is reminiscent of both the lower and higher degrees of Masonry.

COURTYARD, THE UNIVERSITY OF BOLOGNA

Enough of these traditions and legends have grown up about the Order for a dozen more degrees for degree makers. A few of them, referring to familiar symbols of the Fraternity may be here explained. Lorenzo de Medici, "Il Magnifico," who was a patron of the Order in its beginning, adopted the caduceus, an

INTERIOR OF THE CAMPO SANTO
Bologna's Westminster Abbey

emblem of Mercury, as his private seal. Hence the use of the emblem by Kappa Sigma, and name of the magazine of the Fraternity. The motto of the University of Bologna was *Bononia docet mundum* or *Bononia docet*. This is the open motto of Kappa Sigma, and suggests the mission which Kappa Sigma hopes to realize in the new world as Bologna did in the old.

Referring to the traditional origin, Alexander Yerger Scott, of Mississippi, the Conclave orator, at the Grand Conclave at Lookout Mountain, 1906, said:

"We are here, gathered together from the furthest confines of our beloved country; from the North, the East, the West and the South, actuated by like desires, centered upon a single purpose

KAPPA SIGMA HOUSE, MICHIGAN

and inspired by identical ideas and ideals; and that which inspires us, the good we seek, is not selfish but unselfish, not personal, but impersonal, and is represented to us by a name—that name, Kappa Sigma.

"It is this I would have you consider with me. Kappa Sigma is known to the outside world as a college fraternity, a secret organization for boys; a thing for their amusement; a passing phase of youthful experience and pleasure. You and I know differently of Kappa Sigma, whatever may be said of others, for we have within our hearts the esoteric teachings of our beloved Fraternity, and we know it is something more, much more, than a thing to amuse a schoolboy, and to be discarded with the toga.

KAPPA SIGMA HOUSE, O. S. U.

We know that Kappa Sigma represents within itself, and stands for, the great truth that, express it how or when or where we will, from the first dawn of recorded history—aye, beyond that, turn we back the pages of the eternal ages and dip into the past as we will—resolves itself into this, the Fatherhood of God and the Brotherhood of Man.

"Our fraternity rests not its foundation upon recorded history. We cannot, with exactitude, say when nor where nor how the thing we call Kappa Sigma had its birth, any more than we can say when the light first begins to break over a darkened world; nor when nor where man first became a living, breathing spirit reflecting the qualities of Deity. Looking back into the dim past, we find this central truth of life first expressed in myth and in symbol; in the esoteric teachings of eastern religions, the Zend Avestas, the Dhammapodas, the Vedas, the Koran; in the Bibles of the men that have come and gone; in the myths of Greece and Rome; in the Sagas of the Northmen; and the tradi-

KAPPA SIGMA HOUSE, NEW YORK

tions of savages express in some form the same idea—enmeshed, it may be, in much that is unbelievable, much that is absurd to our modern scientific mind. So the central truth of Kappa Sigma comes to us like the central truth of life—through legend and through tradition.

"Tradition—did you ever think what a tradition is; its power, its value, its utility? Traditions are not made by any man, but by time alone. A tradition cannot be proved. It cannot be disproved. It rests alone upon faith—belief—and that is the power of tradition, for faith is the greatest power in all the universe. . . .

"Happy, then, that nation and that people who believe. That their tradition be true or false, reasonable or unreasonable, is of little moment, so that it is believed.

"My brothers, do you realize that Kappa Sigma shares with the Masonry the privileges of having a traditional origin, and that these two secret orders, so far as I know, are the only two that cannot point with historic accuracy to the date of their founding, without resort to tradition—to a time beyond which their written history extends—for a beginning? The Masons date their origin

KAPPA SIGMA HOUSE, STANFORD

at the building of King Solomon's temple, and the sole and only proofs they have of this tradition are the esoteric teachings in their ritual. What one of you does not know that this tradition—fable, if you please to call it—has made Masonry the greatest secret organization the world has ever known? whose power for good is written upon the history of more than one nation, and because of which it is destined, yet, to endure so long as man himself endures.

"How account you for the marvelous growth of Kappa Sigma, for the loving devotion each of us has for the Star and Crescent,

the emblem of our order? Among the youngest of college fraternities in America, it stands to-day the greatest. Can you doubt for
one moment that the living force behind its advance is bound up
in its traditional history? If so, open the floodgates of memory
and recall how your soul was filled with rapture as the story of
her founding was gradually unfolded to you—how, as you learned

KAPPA SIGMA HOUSE, OREGON

the truths taught, as you journeyed towards the City of Letters,
a new light and a new life seemed to fill your youthful heart. You
were at one with the youth of a bygone age. You shared in spirit
the toil and travail of those who, when ignorance, like a pall of
death, had settled upon the world, struggled amid the vicissitudes
of a crime-ridden nation for light and for truth. And it was then

you learned in a new and forceful manner, your duty to your fellow men, the eternal principle of brotherhood, of justice and of love.

"Ah, my friends, through this tradition you'and I seem, some way and somehow, linked to the brave spirits of that day, who sought to defy the power of might with the power of right; who sought to bring out of darkest night a resplendent day, who

KAPPA SIGMA HOUSE, MINNESOTA

wrought for others, knowing full well that one can only reach the full measure of greatness by serving his fellow men. I urge you, then, with all the power at my command, to cling to, believe in and live up to this hallowed tradition of Kappa Sigma that comes to us out of the dim past like the first faint breath of spring time, and which, somehow and some way, makes us better and nobler and stronger because thereof.

"But I like to think that the God of nations and of men held in reserve, from the beginning, another noble mission for our Fraternity—the mission of aiding in binding up and healing the wounds of a nation—and it has ever seemed to me that Kappa Sigma's refounding, after it has winged its gentle way across the dread Atlantic, was prophetic of its mission and lends verity to its early legends.

"Thirty-seven years ago, in the little village of Charlottesville,

KAPPA SIGMA HOUSE, PURDUE

nestling in a beautiful valley of the Alleghenies, within the shadows of Monticello, the historic home of America's greatest commoner, amid the classic columns and colonnades of the University inspired by his genius, our beloved fraternity was born again. The boom of the cannon at Appomattox still reverberates in the distance. Fraternal blood yet crimsons Virginia's tragic soil. Where peace and plenty had found their wonted home, poverty was abroad in the land. Fields, once molten with billowy oceans of golden grain, languidly rolling as the gentle southern zephyrs

UNIVERSITY
OF
CALIFORNIA

played hide and seek mid their million glittering tassels, now lay fallow, silently pleading for the dominion of the plow. Palatial homes, where once the lute made glad music 'neath the southern summer skies, and silvery laughter rippled from merry lips, and beaming eyes flashed with love and life, now lay in smouldering ruins. Eyes that had sparkled were dull with tears. Hearts that had burgeoned and blossomed with love now shrivelled with bitterest hate. War, grim-visaged and dread, had stalked throughout the land for four long years, and all was desolation—all was ruin. And yet it was there, amid these scenes, that our beloved Kappa Sigma had its new birth. It was in the halls of our Fraternity that a part of the youth of the country began to close the doors of the four years of hell this people had lived. There we began to learn that love and not hate, peace and not war, are the laws of life—to know that there was no North and no South, but one great country; that there was no Northerner, no Southerner, but all Americans, blood of the same blood, bone of the same bone, brothers in truth and in fact, united in indissoluble union.

"And so my brothers, on behalf of Kappa Sigma in the South, I welcome you with all my heart. We know one another and we love one another, for Kappa Sigma is Love."

EXTENSION OF THE FRATERNITY

Unlike many fraternities and most of those which originated in the South, Kappa Sigma was never intended to be a sectional fraternity. The men who founded her at the University of Virginia in 1869 were not of small ideas. When Founder McCormick and other founders from Baltimore returned to that city from the university in 1870, they engaged splendid apartments on Lombard Street for fraternity purposes. Here was to be the Alpha Chapter, at the South's old medical school, the University of Maryland. But the time was inopportune, and the Chapter did not make its appearance till 1875, when Dr. A. C. Heffenger, (Zeta) later to be passed assistant surgeon in the navy, an eminent writer and medico-legal expert, initiated a number of gentlemen. In 1871, when Founders Arnold and North went to Bellevue, New York, they were given powers by the parent Chapter to initiate Dr. Henry Seeley Welch, of San Francisco, which they accordingly did. Dr. Welch was to install a Chapter at the University of California, but he also found the time inopportune. Under a similar dispensation, it was in New York at Bellevue, that Dr. George Wyatt Hollingsworth (Beta) was initiated to establish Beta at the University of Alabama, the second Chapter. It should be noted that there were no fraternities at this time at California nor at Alabama—the beginning of the wise policy of extension of Kappa Sigma. There were also hopes of a Chapter in New York City, to be called New York Delta, and to draw its members from all New York City colleges—another brilliant scheme of the dashing Dr. Arnold. Thus of the first four Chapters contemplated, one was in the far South at Alabama, one in the middle tier of states at Maryland, one in

KAPPA SIGMA FRATERNITY

New York, and one on the Pacific—all of which were at a later day to come into existence in the most national, from a geographical standpoint, of all the fraternities.

It was not, however, until 1873, that the mother Chapter took up the extension movement in earnest. In that year a Chapter was placed by Dr. James H. Durham at Trinity College, North Carolina, drawing its members mainly from the old Hesperian Society of that college. From that day to this, time has wit-

HEADQUARTERS AT BROWN
A section of this Dormitory is occupied by Kappa Sigma only

nessed a continual increase in the number of Chapters and the annals of Kappa Sigma, one of the youngest of the great college societies, have been no less brilliant than those of any other Greek letter organization.

It was but natural that the Fraternity should first plant successful Chapters in the South, for there were the friends and kinsmen of its members. Besides, the war had disrupted nearly all college organizations in that section, the field for the running was open to Kappa Sigma equally with older fraternities, the colleges were of the high type of the old-time classical discipline, and fraternity material in the Southern homes of the most intensely thoroughbred of Americans was of the best. Notable as are the founders for their connections, so also may this be remarked of all the Fraternity's early members, for no society had brethren of higher social status than did Kappa Sigma in all her early years. Among those who assisted in building up the organization may be found the sons of such men as Presidents John Tyler and Jefferson Davis, Generals Albert Sidney Johnston, Joe Wheeler, Walker, Taliaferro, Wright, and Stubblefield, of the Confederate armies; Governors Ligon, of Maryland, Walker

KAPPA SIGMA HOUSE, COLORADO MINES

of Virginia, Marks of Tennessee, McLaurin of Mississippi, Berry of Arkansas, and many others. The chapter rolls of the first Southern Chapters are rosters of the names of the first families of the South. A number were the sons of men prominent in the history of other fraternities.

Before Kappa Sigma had a Northern Chapter, she had eleven institutional seats in the South—at Virginia, the keystone of Southern education, with its graduates influencing America, the Harvard of the South; Alabama, whose sons have illustrated the history of the state; Trinity, the favored child of North Carolina

Methodism; Emory and Henry, beloved of Virginia Methodism; Washington and Lee, with its famous graduates in all sections of the history of the South, the West, and the nation, and loved almost as is Virginia; Virginia Military Institute, the "West Point of the South;" Virginia Polytechnic Institute, the first technical school in the South; Maryland, one of the oldest of American medical schools and most popular; Mercer, representative of

KAPPA SIGMA HOUSE, ILLINOIS

the Baptists in the lower South; Vanderbilt, prosperous and favored of a rich benefactor; Tennessee, the sucessor of Blount College, one of the oldest colleges of the South. All of these Chapters save Virginia Polytechnic, Emory and Henry, and Virginia Military Institute are alive to-day, and these three were killed only by anti-fraternity laws. The founders knew well how to cultivate vitality and to choose institutions. All of these and our later Southern Kappa Sigma colleges are adornments to our Chapter roll.   Their history is a part of the history of America, and an inspiration.   In some cases their incomes and student bodies are not so large as some of their newer Northern and Western sisters.   Yet their buildings and equipment are of the best, for, following the classical courses, they do not need large sums for technical apparatus, and their professors are willing to work for a spiritual reward.   The tone of their student

KAPPA SIGMA HOUSE, CASE

bodies is unexcelled in the United States.   With the prosperity of the new South, even many are becoming rich in money.

The only period not of the highest prosperity known to the Fraternity was the college generation of four years from 1880 to 1884.   This was due to no lack of interest among Kappa Sigmas, but to a peculiarly sad and universal condition of a lack of prosperity of Kappa Sigma colleges in the unsettled condition of the

South, and to assaults, by anti-fraternity laws, on Kappa Sigma Chapters.

In the movement into Southern colleges, the name of the immortal Kappa Sigma, Stephen Alonzo Jackson—"Lon Jackson"— is enshrined in the heart of every Kappa Sig. The son of a banker, a mystic, an idealist. and advanced in Masonry, this

STEPHEN ALONZO JACKSON

golden-hearted Virginian ruined his fortune in behalf of the Order. "S. A. Jackson Day," the fourth of March, was ordered to be regularly observed among Kappa Sigmas, by the Richmond Grand Conclave of 1894.

It was not until 1880 that Kappa Sigma established a Chapter in the North. Then it was that a number of the members of the Zeta Epsilon literary society at Lake Forest petitioned for

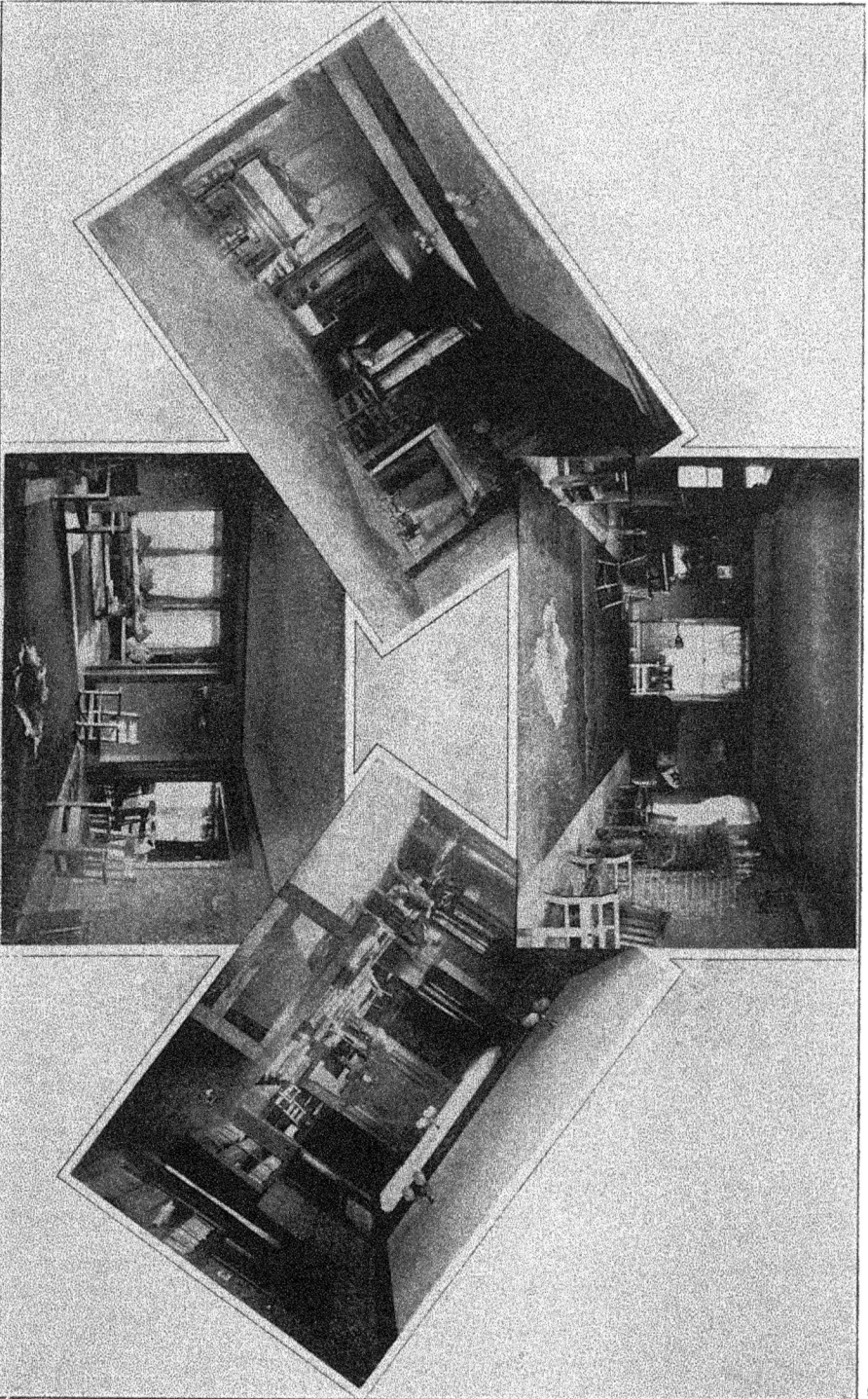

INTERIORS, CORNELL AND STANFORD KAPPA SIGMA HOUSES

and received a charter. This was the first Northern Chapter of
a fraternity of Southern origin. The Chapter survived only till
1882, for knowledge of membership in it meant expulsion from
the college. A second petition for a Chapter at another Northern
college was received from an organization which had withdrawn
from its general fraternity, but this petition was rejected. In

KAPPA SIGMA HOUSE, LAKE FOREST

1885, a Chapter was organized at Purdue. From this point on-
ward is a history of the conquest of the North and West. The
Fraternity now has the longest roll of all the fraternities—seven-
ty-six Chapters. It has the widest geographical distribution of
the fraternities, being represented in more states of the Union
than any other—having Chapters in thirty-five states, the District of Columbia and the coming state of Oklahoma.

This list shows the order in which Kappa Sigma entered the states and territories, the first Chapter in each, and the date of its foundation: 1. Virginia (Virginia, 1869) ; 2. Alabama (Alabama, 1871) ; 3. North Carolina (Trinity, 1873) ; 4. Maryland (Maryland, 1874) ; 5. Georgia (Mercer, 1875) ; 6. Tennessee (Vanderbilt, 1877) ; 7. Illinois (Lake Forest, 1880) ; 8. West Virginia

KAPPA SIGMA HOUSE, GEORGE WASHINGTON

(West Virginia, 1883) ; 9. Texas (Texas, 1884) ; 10. Indiana (Purdue, 1885) ; 11. Louisiana (Centenary, 1885) ; 12. Maine (Maine, 1886) ; 13. Ohio (Ohio Northern, 1886) ; 14. Pennsylvania (Swarthmore, 1888) ; 15. South Carolina (South Carolina, 1890) ; 16. Arkansas (Arkansas, 1890) ; 17. Michigan (Michigan, 1892) ; 18. District of Columbia (George Washington—formerly known as Columbian—1892) ; 19. New York (Cornell, 1892) ;

20. Vermont (Vermont, 1893) ; 21. Kentucky (Bethel, 1894) ;
22. Mississippi (Millsaps, 1895) ; 23. Nebraska (Nebraska,
1897) ; 24. Missouri (William Jewell, 1897) ; 25. Rhode Island
(Brown, 1898) ; 26. Wisconsin (Wisconsin, 1898) ; 27. California (Stanford, 1898) ; 28. New Hampshire (New Hampshire,
1901) ; 29. Minnesota (Minnesota, 1901) ; 30. Colorado (Denver, 1902) ; 31. Iowa (Iowa, 1902) ; 32. Kansas (Baker, 1903) ;
33. Washington (Washington, 1903) ; 34. Oregon (Oregon,
1904) ; 35. Massachusetts (Massachusetts State, 1904) ; 36. Idaho
(Idaho, 1905) ; 37. Oklahoma (Oklahoma, 1906).

The Fraternity early observed the decadence of many of the old

KAPPA SIGMA HOUSE, MISSOURI

sectarian colleges in the North, where fraternities in the past had
most of their chapters, and shunned them. At the same time,
she prophesied the splendid future of the state institutions—the
result of the congressional acts of 1862 and later—and other
institutions founded since the civil war. Fraternities of Northern
origin in these places had no more prestige due to the age of
their chapters than did Kappa Sigma. The fraternity thus found
opportunities in the North and West similar to those she had
met in the South—the best universities, and these not overcrowded by Greek letter societies. At present in the leading seats of
American educational progress—the state schools, colleges, and

universities—Kappa Sigma has a larger number of Chapters than
any other fraternity. Nearly fifty per cent of them are so located.
She is also represented in all but four of the twenty universities
in the United States having the largest enrollment—Harvard,
Columbia, California, Northwestern, Michigan, Minnesota, Cor-
nell, Illinois, Yale, Chicago, Pennsylvania, Nebraska, Syracuse,
New York, Ohio State, Missouri, Princeton, Indiana, George
Washington and Stanford. Of these four—Princeton, Columbia,
Northwestern and Yale—Princeton does not admit fraternities.
Alumni familiar with the situation in the next two institutions
mentioned, in New York and Chicago respectively, have repeat-

KAPPA SIGMA HOUSE, BAKER

edly advised against entering Columbia or Northwestern. Both
are crowded with fraternities, and conditions at Columbia seem
to demand the ownership of a very costly house to start with.
No movement looking toward Yale has ever received encourage-
ment, for reasons recently expressed by President Hadley of that
university—"A large part of the fraternities are not even known
by their Greek-letter names. . . . When I want to know
what is the Greek-letter name of any organization, I have to look
it up in the Yale *Banner*. Even those societies like Delta Kappa
Epsilon or Psi Upsilon, which have retained their Greek-letter
names in common parlance, are never known as fraternities, but

as societies; and when they go to conventions the delegates have to cram up on purpose to find out what is the grip, or what the Greek-letters stand for, or any other supposed secrets of the fraternity."

Kappa Sigma was the pioneer fraternity of Southern origin in the seven Northern states of Maine, New Hampshire, Illinois, Indiana, Wisconsin, West Virginia and Minnesota. This does not take into account the powers extended to Dr. George Miles Arnold in 1871, by the Virginia Chapter to initiate from New York City colleges. Kappa Sigma has been the pioneer fra-

KAPPA SIGMA HOUSE, PENNSYLVANIA

ternity of Southern origin in fifteen Northern colleges: Bowdoin, Case, Dartmouth, Illinois, Indiana, Lake Forest, Maine, Minnesota, New Hampshire, New York, Purdue, Swarthmore, Syracuse, West Virginia, and Wisconsin. She has been the second oldest fraternity of Southern origin in a number of Northern institutions, having been preceded by Alpha Tau Omega at Brown, Pennsylvania, Vermont and Washington and Jefferson; and similarly preceded by Sigma Alpha Epsilon at Harvard, Bucknell and Dickinson, and by Sigma Nu at the University of Iowa. An examination of the history of Kappa Sigma's Chapter roll—North, South, and West—shows that at present or at some time in their careers, twenty-two of her Chapters are or have been the first chapters founded or the oldest chapters on account of continuous existence in their respective universities.

Many Chapters have been formed from local and other societies, thus giving a Chapter an element of stability at its inception, this policy being as marked in Kappa Sigma as in any other fraternity. Yet it has never sought to add the names of United States senators and other prominent men to its alumni lists by enrolling them without initiation or active affiliation—an abuse in some fraternities. Indeed, conservatism in this regard led to the breaking off of negotiations for union of Kappa Sigma with two other general fraternities. Until 1902, the initiation of alumni of local societies was prohibited; since then under certain restrictions it has been permitted. Those Chapters formed from other societies are: Emory and Henry (Phi Mu Omicron),[1] Washington and Lee, as reestablished in 1904 (Mu Pi Lambda),[2] Lake Forest (Lambda Phi),[3] Grant, as reestablished (The Secret Fraternity); Hampden-Sidney (Phi Mu Gamma); Maine (K. K. F.—Roman letter); Bucknell (Phi Ep-

---

[1] Some of the members of the Emory and Henry chapter and several members of other chapters of Phi Mu Omicron were admitted into Kappa Sigma in 1879. This society was founded at South Carolina College in 1858, and is the second oldest of the defunct societies of Southern origin. It also had chapters at Wofford, Charleston, Emory, Newberry, and Emory and Henry. Its badge was a monogram of the letters comprising the name of the society. Members of the *first* southern Kappa Alpha joined Phi Mu Omicron in 1866. *Kukloi Adelphon* or "circles" flourished as select organizations among the southern gentry before the war in the colleges and also in the "court" towns or county seats in Alabama, Virginia, Kentucky and other southern states. After the war, in the Reconstruction period, these *kukloi* formed a basis for the Ku Klux Klan.

[2] The Washington and Lee chapter of Mu Pi Lambda was the mother chapter of that fraternity, founded in 1895, and also having chapters at Virginia, Harvard, West Virginia, and William and Mary. At Jefferson's home, "Monticello," Virginia, in 1904, the society disbanded. The William and Mary chapter joined Theta Delta Chi; part of the Virginia chapter joined Phi Delta Theta and Kappa Sigma. Its badge was a five-sided shield displaying the letters, Mu Pi Lambda, beneath an eye and above the skull and bones. It published a quarterly, the *Archon.*

[3] Lambda Phi was a continuation of the well-known "Suicide Club" of Lake Forest.

silon); William Jewell (Pi Alpha Theta); New Hampshire
(Q. T. V.);[4] Minnesota (Alpha Theta); California (Beta Kappa
Delta); Denver (Kappa Delta); Dickinson (Pi Gamma Alpha);
Iowa (Phi Upsilon); Baker (Skull and Bones); Case (Phi Alpha
Chi); Colorado (Phi Psi Sigma); Chicago (Bronze Shield);
Massachusetts State (D. G. K.);[5] Dartmouth (Beta Gamma);
Harvard (Pi Upsilon); Idaho (Sigma Delta Alpha); Oklahoma
(Alpha Delta Sigma).

When the Michigan Chapter was founded its membership was at
first confined to the law school, similar to Sigma Chi in that
University.

The few and short periods of inactivity of Kappa Sigma Chapters are remarkable to contemplate. Of the large fraternities
having over fifty Chapters, Kappa Sigma has the smallest percentage of dead or inactive Chapters. A number of the Chapters
have become victims of anti-fraternity legislation. Those at Virginia Military Institute, Emory and Henry and the Virginia
Polytechnic Institute were forced out through these regulations.
The Alabama Chapter was killed by anti-fraternity laws shortly
after its foundation, and was revived in 1899. Hostile legislation
caused the inactivity of the Vanderbilt Chapter from 1880 to
1885, although anti-fraternity laws prevailed from the foundation
of the university in 1875. The Lake Forest Chapter was also
inactive on account of hostile legislation from 1882 to 1896. The
inactivity of the South Carolina Chapter commenced with Senator
Ben Tillman's anti-fraternity legislation in the South Carolina
Legislature in 1897.

Exclusiveness caused the Washington and Lee Chapter to be-

[4] Q. T. V. was the first technical fraternity to have more than one chapter, being founded at Massachusetts State College, in 1869. It had chapters at Massachusetts State, Maine, New Hampshire, Pennsylvania State, Worcester Polytechnic and Cornell. The Pennsylvania State chapter joined Phi Kappa Sigma and the Maine chapter joined Phi Gamma Delta. The fraternity published a handsome quarto journal from Boston and a catalogue in 1886. The badge was a diamond-shaped slab upon which is engraved a monogram of the letters "Q. T. V."

[5] This society, established in 1868 at Massachusetts State, was the first technical fraternity ever founded. It published a catalogue in 1879 and issued for many years an annual called the *Cycle,* which it continues.

come inactive in 1877. It was reestablished in 1888, but with the overcrowded condition of the institution, fraternities pledging men on incoming trains, it was withdrawn in 1900. It was again installed in 1904 by the absorption of the mother Chapter of Mu Pi Lambda. The Chapter at the University of Maryland was withdrawn in 1875 on account of an unseemly conflict with the Rush Medical Society of that University. It was revived in 1890 with the privilege of drawing membership from both Maryland

THE LIVING ROOM, KAPPA SIGMA HOUSE, HARVARD

and Johns Hopkins universities, but was again withdrawn because of the laxity of organization from which city Chapters suffer. It was revived in 1898 and from that date has been very successful. By agreement, all fraternities, owing to the fact they were supposed to be ruining the literary societies, withdrew from Trinity in 1879; the Chapter was revived in 1892. The Chapters at Grant and West Virginia were discontinued, the first for lack of material, the second on account of local difficulties. Internal dissensions affecting the Indianapolis or Butler Chapter, caused its withdrawal. The Chapter at Emory College was discontinued on account of failure of members to return to college and the desire of the Fraternity not to remain in the institution, the last Kappa Sigma being valedictorian of his class. Several causes led to the withdrawal of the Indiana Chapter in 1888: the Chapter was reestablished in 1900, and prospers. The Chapter at Centenary was the first established there after the Civil War,

KAPPA SIGMA HOUSE, WISCONSIN

but was withdrawn in 1904 on account of the decline of the college, due to agitation over its removal. The Chapters at Ohio Northern and Thatcher Institute were withdrawn because these colleges were not considered to be up to the full American collegiate standard. The Chapter at Bethel College surrendered its charter on account of lack of suitable material. The Mercer Chapter was withdrawn in 1879 during a wretched period in the college's history, and was installed again in 1891. The Chapter at Kentucky State College is regarded as a continuation of the Chapter at Kentucky University, the latter having been withdrawn on account of the desire not to have two Chapters in the same town. The Chapter at North Georgia College surrendered its charter with a decline of the institution. When the Maryland Military and Naval Academy, the most important military institute of private foundation ever established in the country, was financially wrecked by its officers in 1887, the Chapter there ceased to exist.

The Fraternity's relations with other societies have been cordial. The first numbers in the following give the number of all the Chapters of various fraternities met by Kappa Sigma, and the second numbers the percentage of such Chapters to the entire Chapter roll of each fraternity: Sigma Alpha Epsilon, 45, 68 per cent; Phi Delta Theta, 41, 59 per cent; Sigma Nu, 36, 65 per cent; Beta Theta Pi, 33, 49 per cent; Phi Gamma Delta, 33, 58 per cent; Kappa Alpha (Southern Order), 33, 67 per cent; Sigma Chi, 31, 57 per cent; Delta Tau Delta, 27, 56 per cent; Alpha Tau Omega, 27, 53 per cent; Phi Kappa Psi, 23, 55 per cent; Pi Kappa Alpha, 21, 72 per cent; Phi Kappa Sigma, 18, 72 per cent; Delta Kappa Epsilon, 16, 39 per cent; Delta Upsilon, 16, 44 per cent; Psi Upsilon, 12, 55 per cent; Zeta Psi, 12, 55 per cent; Theta Delta Chi, 12, 50 per cent; Chi Phi, 11, 55 per cent; Chi Psi, 10, 56 per cent; Alpha Delta Phi, 9, 38 per cent; Phi Sigma Kappa, 8, 42 per cent; Sigma Phi Epsilon, 5, 38 per cent; Sigma Phi, 4, 50 per cent; Delta Phi, 4, 36 per cent; Delta Psi, 2, 25 per cent; Kappa Alpha (Northern Order), 2, 29 per cent; Alpha Chi Rho, 2, 33 per cent.

Kappa Sigma has always opposed "lifting," repeatedly refusing propositions of this kind, although when such a practice was considered legitimate, in 1880, it took several members of the Virginia Polytechnic Chapter of Beta Theta Pi, after the Betas had surrendered their charter. However, the giving up of the charter was in no way influenced by Kappa Sigma. The charge that Kappa Sigma lifted the Iowa Chapter of Alpha Chi Rho is unsupported by facts. The Phi Epsilon Society of Bucknell, which became a Chapter of Kappa Sigma, was formed some

KAPPA SIGMA HOUSE, CALIFORNIA

time before by members of Sigma Alpha Epsilon, who had withdrawn, they asserted, for just cause, from the latter fraternity. In 1904, membership in the sophomore society of Theta Nu Epsilon was prohibited. The names of Kappa Sigmas may be found in all other famous inter-class local and professional fraternities.

A Kappa Sigma, Dean Charles W. Burkett of N. C. A. and M., founded the technical fraternity Alpha Zeta. Another Kappa Sigma, Powell C. Fauntleroy, of the U. S. Navy, was one of the founders of Pi Mu, the first medical fraternity of Southern origin. One of the founders of Chi Omega, a prosperous national sorority of Southern origin, was Dr. Charles Richardson, of Arkansas.

The following is the Chapter roll of Kappa Sigma. For more detailed references to it, see Appendix B. In order there are date of foundation, name of Chapter, name of university, date of inactivity and number of initiates to July 1, 1906.

1869. Zeta, University of Virginia 165
1871. Beta, University of Alabama 68
1873. Eta, Trinity College (N. C.) 118
1873. Mu, Washington and Lee University 90
1874. Xi, Virginia Military Institute (1883) 23
1874. Nu, Virginia Polytechnic Institute (1889) 91
1874. Omicron, Emory and Henry College (1895) 138
1874. Alpha-Alpha, University of Maryland 100
1875. Alpha-Beta, Mercer University 93
1877. Kappa, Vanderbilt University 160
1880. Lambda, University of Tennessee 192
1880. Alpha Chi, Lake Forest University 68
1882. Alpha Iota, Grant University 43
1882. Phi, Southwestern Presbyterian University 116
1882. Omega, University of the South 175
1883. Pi, University of West Virginia (1887) 17
1883. Upsilon, Hampden-Sidney College 94
1884. Tau, University of Texas 205
1885. Rho, North Georgia Agricultural College (1891)..... 32
1885. Chi, Purdue University 166
1885. Delta, Maryland Military and Naval Academy (1887) 31
1885. Epsilon, Centenary College (1904) 84
1886. Psi, University of Maine 180
1886. Sigma, Ohio Northern University (1888) 23

6

1901. Beta-Nu, Kentucky State College 40
1901. Beta-Xi, University of California 48
1902. Beta-Omicron, University of Denver 40
1902. Beta-Pi, Dickinson College 45
1902. Beta-Sigma, Washington University (Mo.) 32
1902. Beta-Rho, University of Iowa 58
1903. Beta-Tau, Baker University 49
1903. Beta-Upsilon, North Carolina A. and M. College 42
1903. Beta-Phi, Case School of Applied Science 41
1903. Beta-Chi, Missouri School of Mines 29
1903. Beta-Psi, University of Washington 32
1904. Beta-Omega, Colorado College 28
1904. Gamma-Alpha, University of Oregon 28
1904. Gamma-Beta, University of Chicago 26
1904. Gamma-Gamma, Colorado School of Mines 29
1904. Gamma-Delta, Massachusetts State College 101
1905. Gamma-Zeta, New York University 15
1905. Gamma-Epsilon, Dartmouth College 32
1905. Gamma-Eta, Harvard University 29
1905. Gamma-Theta, University of Idaho 29
1906. Gamma-Iota, Syracuse University 18
1906. Gamma-Kappa, University of Oklahoma 12

Number of active Chapters, 76; inactive Chapters, 15; number of initiates, 7155.

STATISTICS OF KAPPA SIGMA COLLEGES.

COLLEGE.	LOCATION.	Date of Opening.	Control.	Number of Students.	Income.	Value of equipment in buildings, appa- ratus, etc., exclusive of permanent in- come funds.
University of Maine	Orono, Me.	1867	State	426	96,00	351,845
Bowdoin College	Brunswick, Me.	1802	Cong.	391	85,358	1,008,500
New Hampshire College	Durham, N. H.	1868	State	200	136,457	275,00
...th College	Hanover, N. H.	1769	Cg.	815	146,900	1,478,797
University of Vermont	Burlington, Vt.	1800	Sate	566	98,359	875,200
...ts State College	Amherst, Mass.	1867	State	175	164,444	358,723
Harvard University	Cambridge, Mss.	1638	..t.	5,136	1,509,533	6,900,000
Brown University	Providence, R. I.	1764	Bapt.	940	192,832	2,385,000
...ell University	Ithaca, N. Y.	1868	N- set.	3,457	1,214,334	4,252,522
New York ..y	New York, N. Y.	1831	..t.	2,211	252,126	2,422,820
Syracuse University	Syracuse, N. Y.	1871	M. E.	2,009	281,878	1,473,874
Swarthmore College	Swarthmore, Pa.	1869	Friends	209	80,893	391,500
Pennsylvania State College	State College Pa.	1859	State	568	144,226	950,000
University of Pennsylvania	...a, Pa.	1740	..t.	2,578	588,703	6,896,093
Bucknell University	Lewisburg, Pa.	1846	Bapt.	633	369,000	.....
Lehigh University	...th ...m, Pa.	1866	Non-sect.	581	95,000	1,450,000
Dickinson College	Carlisle, Pa.	1783	M. E.	481	79,505	489,000
University of Maryland	Baltimore, Md.	1812	Non sect.	825	.....	.....
George Washington University	Washington, D. C.	1821	Bapt.	1,298	105,144	946,120
University of ...	...le, Va.	1825	State	605	157,159	1,348,500
Randolph-...n College	Ashland, Va.	1832	M. E. So.	127	21,667	145,000
Washington and Lee ...	Lexington, Va.	1749	Non sect.	279	57,00	350,000
William and Mary College	Williamsburg, Va.	1693	State	165	24,382	47,00
Hampden-Sidney College	Hampden Sidney, Va.	1776	Presb.	94	13,400	172,00

COLLEGE.	LOCATION.	Date of Opening.	Control.	Number of Students.	Income.	Value of equipment in buildings, apparatus, etc., exclusive of permanent income funds.
...d College	...d, Va	1832	Bapt.	210	....	631,000
Davidson College	Davidson, N.C.	1837	Presb.	225	20,000	202,000
Trinity College	Durham, N C	1851	M.E. S.	364	34,446	497,342
...ity of ...th	...el Hill, N. C.	1795	tSte	698	89,750	500,000
...rth Carolina A. and M ...ge	W. Raleigh, N C	1889	State	505	123,548	257,965
Wofford College	...g, S. C.	1854	M. E. So.	297	17,584	250,000
...r University	...n, G.	1837	Bapt.	222	17,000	213,000
Georgia School of Technology	...a, Ga.	1888	State	483	61,500	254,000
...sity of Georgia	...s, Ga.	1801	State	359	187,705	540,890
University of Alabama	...ty, Ala.	1831	Ste	375	50,200	255,000
...a Polytechnic Institute	...n, Ala.	1872	State	435	70,335	231,000
...d University	...a, Tenn.	1842	Presb.	217	11,420	150,000
...ilt University	...le, Tenn.	1875	M. E. So.	691	130,000	1,025,000
...ity of Tennessee	Knoxville, Tenn.	1794	State	756	97,232	613,290
Southwestern Presbyterian Univers.	Clarksville, ...n.	1855	Presb.	91	17,383	106,000
...ity of the South	..., Tenn.	1868	P. E.	517	52,036	670,396
Southwestern Baptist University	...n, Tenn.	1847	Bapt.	288	12,700	58,500
...o S...	...ns, ...io	1873	State Mt.	1,717	499,393	2,940,000
...e School of Applied Science	...ld, G.	1881		479	....	591,000
...n ...d Jefferson College	...n, Pa.	1802	Presb.	349	37,769	365,000
Kentucky S...e College	Lexington, Ky.	1866	State	696	114,827	637,578
University of Michigan	Am A..., M...	1837	State	3,792	782,283	3,300,000
Purdue University	Lafayette, Ind	1874	State	1,339	234,610	635,750
Wash College	...le, Ind	1832	Presb.	203	33,000	715,000
...ity of ...ia	Bloomington, Ind	1824	State	1 49	190,482	335,000
...ity of Illinois	Urbana, Ill.	1868	State	3,288	574,731	1,665,000

COLLEGE.	LOCATION.	Date of Opening.	Control.	Number of Students.	Income.	Value of equipment in buildings, apparatus, etc., exclusive of permanent income funds.
Lake Forest University	Lake Forest, Ill	1858	Presb.	313	127,300	750,000
University of ...	Chicago, Ill	1892	...	4,463	982,610	6,392,188
... of ...	..., Wis	1850	State	2,870	60,878	2,056,47
... of ...	..., Minn	1868	State	3,788	516,336	1,973,60
University of Iowa	Iowa City, Iowa	1847	State	1,442	435,000	1,307,350
... of ...	..., Neb	1869	State	2,560	251,738	1,015,00
William ... College	..., Mo	1849	Bapt.	365	22,000	160,000
... State University	..., Mo	1841	State	1,591	573,582	1,400,00
... School of ...	St. Louis, Mo	1859	Non-sect	2,229	90,000	2,275,00
...	Rolla, Mo	1871	State	225	......	......
Baker University	..., Kas	1858	M. E.	907	30,000	180,000
... of ...	..., Ark	1872	State	896	101,787	476,000
... of ...	..., Fla	1892	...	465	79,000	92,003
... College	..., Miss	1892	M. E. S.	258	13,500	108,500
... State University	..., La	1860	State	424	148,892	364,038
... University	New Orleans, La	1834	Non-sect	1,366	142,000	1,083,000
... University	..., Tex	1873	M. E. So	417	25,119	315,000
Southwestern University	Austin, Tex	1883	State	1,437	230,303	90,00
... University	University Park, Colo	1864	M. E.	1,361	59,733	445,000
Colorado College	Golden, Colo	1874	Cong.	529	44,600	517,463
Colorado School of Mines	..., Colo	1874	State	214	78,719	251,413
Leland Stanford, Jr., University	Stanford University, Cal	1891	Non-sect	1,483	696,000	2,280,000
University of California	Berkeley, Cal	1869	State	3,887	653,327	2,340,000
University of Oregon	..., Ore	1862	State	631	75,000	817,000
University of Idaho	Moscow, Idaho	1876	State	447	61,558	167,000
...	..., Idaho	1892	State	353	113,398	29,90

While Kappa Sigma is proud of her sons who are distinguished in the country's intellectual, political and material life of her Chapter roll of famous institutions, of her enthusiastic graduate clubs, yet she has always emphasized the fraternal harmony and fellowship, and high ideals, that mark a Kappa Sigma brother, wherever you may find one, throughout life, until death. While some fraternities count their disloyal members by dozens and even by Chapters, Kappa Sigma has had but a few isolated cases where an undergraduate left the Fraternity to join another. These separate cases occurred a number of years ago in the North, while the Fraternity was young.

Thus, this congenial society of scholars and gentlemen do not allow their fraternal associations to die when they leave their universities. Good-fellowship, and not scholastic pedantry alone, was emphasized by the American founders. There are Alumni Clubs all over the country where dinners and dances keep up a delightful friendship. Toasts to Kappa Sigma have been heard at dinner at all the famous resorts from the Palace Hotel in San Francisco to the Waldorf-Astoria in New York and from the Auditorium in Chicago to the St. Charles in New Orleans. Many of these events are becoming traditional, such as the "Norfolk Fish Fry," the "Dutch Treat" at Denver, the "French Dinner" at San Francisco, the "Round Table" at Washington, the "Thanksgiving Dinner" at Kansas City, the "New England Initiation Dinner" at Boston, the "New York Annual," the "Philadelphia Dinner," the "Big Chicago Dinner," the "Danville New Year's Dinner," and many more. In many of the leading cities—St. Louis, Los Angeles, Seattle, New York, Chicago, Salt Lake, New Orleans, San Francisco, Washington, Denver, Boston, Pittsburgh and possibly others—it is customary for Kappa Sigmas to meet once a week for lunch in some selected restaurant in the center of the business district.

There are now Alumni Chapters at

Atlanta	Milwaukee
Birmingham	Mobile
Boston	Montgomery
Buffalo	Nashville
Chattanooga	New Orleans
Chicago	New York
Concord	Norfolk
Covington	Philadelphia
Danville, Ill.	Pine Bluff
Danville, Va.	Pittsburg
Denver	Portland
Durham	Richmond
Fort Smith	Ruston
Indianapolis	St. Louis
Ithaca	Salt Lake City
Jackson, Miss.	San Francisco
Jackson, Tenn.	Savannah
Kansas City	Seattle
Kinston	Texarkana
Little Rock	Vicksburg
Los Angeles	Waco
Louisville	Washington
Lynchburg	Wilmington
Memphis	Yazoo City

The alumni spirit once caused an Alumni Chapter to be formed without the confines of the United States, at Chihuahua, Mexico, the first foreign alumni chapter of any fraternity. At one time there were state associations of the Chapters and alumni of Tennessee, Louisiana, Texas and Virginia, but these were abandoned when the District system was adopted. A club-house, the first of its kind at Washington, D. C., was supported by the alumni of that city during 1902 and 1903. It was successful, but was temporarily given up in order that a club building more central-

ly located in the club district might be obtained, a task almost im-
possible. The University of Maryland house is used with and
supported jointly by the alumni of Baltimore as a club-house for
the latter. The New York alumni are now forming a corporation
to acquire and furnish a club-house; such New York clubs have

KAPPA SIGMA HOUSE, MARYLAND

been successful with at least two fraternities. Boston alumni
are considering a similar scheme.

The accompanying map shows the number of Kappa Sigmas in
each state and also every town where a Kappa Sigma may be located. No one section can claim a monopoly of them. Notice

how Pennsylvania and Texas balance each other, or New York and Mississippi, or Illinois and Georgia.

Membership in the Fraternity is restricted. No one may be initiated unless he be a member of the college where there is a Chapter. In one case, the general Fraternity conferred honorary membership, and thereby honored itself, upon Jefferson Davis,

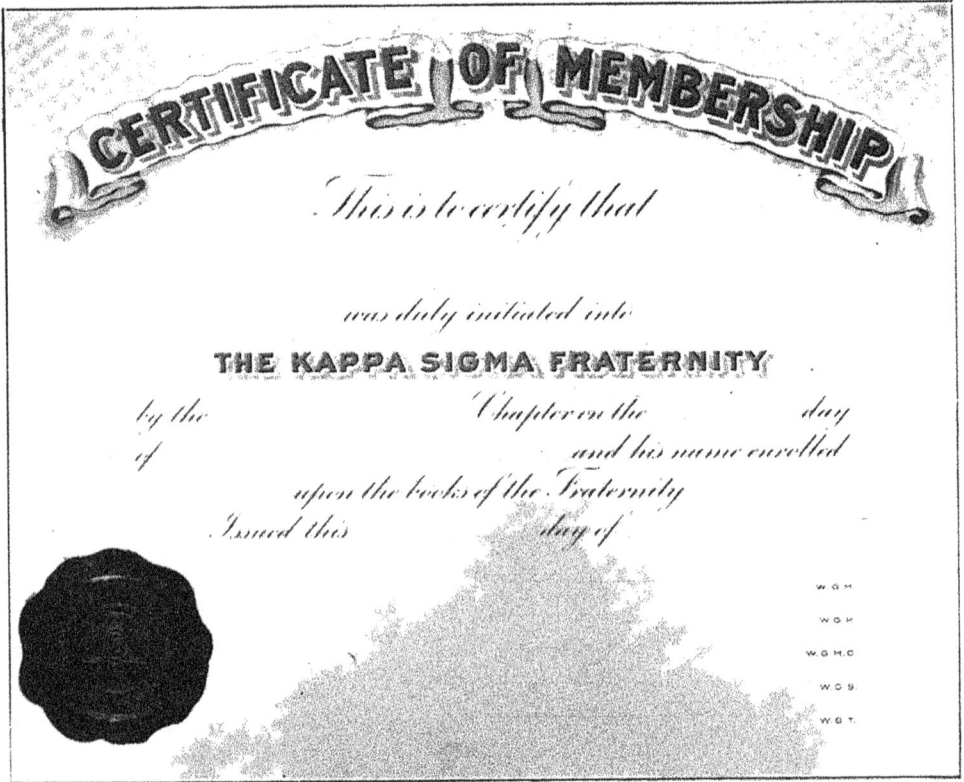

FORM OF KAPPA SIGMA MEMBERSHIP CERTIFICATE

president of the Confederate States of America. The President's son, Jefferson Davis, Jr., was a member at Virginia Military Institute. The president and his family have always had a peculiarly tender affection for the Fraternity. To both Mrs. Davis and Miss Winnie Davis, the general Fraternity has presented badges, and Mrs. Davis was never seen without her Kappa Sigma insignia. Miss Davis' badge was thought to be the most beautiful Greek letter fraternity badge ever produced. However, the

JEFFERSON DAVIS
Kappa Sigma's Only Honorary Member

society is as much Northern as it is Southern. The same Grand Conclave which sent the badge to Mrs. Davis also sent one to Mrs. Grant, widow of the President, whose favorite grandson. Capt. Algernon E. U. Sartoris, is a Kappa Sigma. A number of other scions of the White House are members.

A complete list of the names of prominent alumni would be tiresome. Kappa Sigmas \are to be found in all places where the prizes of American life are being won. There are men of national and international proportions in Wall Street, the Army and Navy, in Congress, as heads of large corporations, college presidents, re-

A GROUP OF "OLD GRADS" RETURNED TO A KAPPA SIGMA HOUSE

formers, railroad officials, State officers, editors of magazines and newspapers, and with world-wide reputations as captains of industry, lawyers, physicians and litterateurs. Kappa Sigma, so thoroughly American, views with a special pride its record in the Spanish-American war, wherein, according to the publications of other fraternities, it had a larger percentage of men engaged in proportion to its membership than any other Greek letter organization. There were Kappa Sigmas from privates to general officers. True to its ancient literary origin in Europe, members of the Order established the first English newspaper in the Philippines and the first all-English newspaper in Cuba.

T H E   G O V E R N M E N T

The Fraternity was first governed by Zeta, or the mother Chapter, at the University of Virginia. In July, 1876, a Grand Conclave was called at the old Eutaw House, Baltimore. Here was instituted the Supreme Executive Committee, a body of legislative, judicial, and executive powers. Greater authority was added to it by the Richmond, Virginia, Conclave, in October, 1878. During a period in 1884, the Committee was relieved of much purely secretarial work when Omega Chapter, at the University of the South attended to much detail as a grand Chapter. But from 1878 to the present there has been a government not precisely similar to that of any other college fraternity. Many have a central body similar to the Supreme Executive Committee. Following what is known as the "Masonic tradition"—for Masonry makes its officers supreme—hardly any other society leaves that governing body so free to act for the best interests of the Fraternity in all things which may come up for consideration between regular Conclaves. The Fraternity, as a whole, responds promptly and cheerfully to the direction of the S. E. C. In fact, this body has wielded more influence and attained better results in several instances in the government of students than college presidents. The Fraternity has come into closer contact with college faculties than any other, for once a year the S. E. C. inquires directly of the college authorities concerning the scholarship and general record of the members of each Chapter, acting upon the replies as may be needed.

Difficulties with faculties over opposition to fraternities are almost things of the past. For years at Emory and Henry, there was an unceasing war. Such was the case at Virginia Polytechnic Institute. At the latter, General Lomax and President Davis, of the Confederacy, were brought into the discussion. The Fraternity faced the obnoxious regulations at the opening of Vanderbilt, for the first year maintaining one of the most successful *sub rosa* chapters ever in existence—as did Phi Delta Theta at a slightly later period—but finally succumbed. Anti-fraternity laws coupled with the rigid military discipline at the "West Point of the South," the Virginia Military Institute, killed the Chapter.

THE EUTAW HOUSE, BALTIMORE
Where the First Grand Conclave was held, 1876

For the first two years at Lake Forest, knowledge of membership meant expulsion from the college. There was trouble over admission of the Fraternity to the University of the South, but the influence of General E. Kirby Smith and President Jefferson Davis, exerted in behalf of Kappa Sigma, made the course possible. The hardest fight ever made in behalf of fraternities in American colleges has taken place in Arkansas where the contest has been carried, under the leadership of the Arkansas Chap-

ter and its alumni, into the legislature.   The result is still in the balance. ·

The records of the various offices of the Fraternity are very complete and voluminous.   By the use of blank forms for reports to and from the Chapters, they have been highly systematized and brought up to the latest methods.   It has been the policy of the Fraternity to train certain of the officers of the S. E. C. as specialists, and these have held their positions for years.   Even

BUSINESS OFFICE OF KAPPA SIGMA, DANVILLE, VIRGINIA

with their complete knowledge of the Fraternity's workings, they are compelled to devote almost half their time to it—practically a labor of love with them.

The members of the Supreme Executive Committee are a Worthy Grand Master, a Worthy Grand Procurator, a Worthy Grand Master of Ceremonies, a Worthy Grand Scribe and a Worthy Grand Treasurer.   The other national officers are a songbook editor, a catalogue editor, a historian and an alumni secretary.

REV. FINIS KING FARR, D.D., W.G.M. OF KAPPA SIGMA

HON. JOHN RANDOLPH NEAL, W.G.P. OF KAPPA SIGMA

JEREMIAH SWEETSER FERGUSON, M.D., W.G.M.C. OF KAPPA SIGMA

HERBERT MILTON MARTIN, ESQ., W.G.S. OF KAPPA SIGMA

MAJOR STANLEY WATKINS MARTIN, W.G.T. OF KAPPA SIGMA

THE SUPREME EXECUTIVE COMMITTEES OF KAPPA SIGMA.

	W.G.M.	W.G.P.	W.G.M.C.	W.G.S.	W.G.T.
1876-8	S A Jackson	Office not created	Office not created	W. F. Page	W. F. Page
1878-80	S. A. Jackson	L. G. Tyler	Office not created	W. F. Page	W. F. Page
1880-3	H. M. Smith, Jr	S. A. Jackson	Office not created	W. T. Page / W. G. McAdoo	S. P. Withers. / W. G. McAdoo / A. M. Moulton.
1883-5	W. G. McAdoo / W. H. Inglesby	S. A. Jackson	W I Thomas	W. H. Inglesby / E. A. Snowden	E. W. Hughes.
1885-7	S. A. Jackson	W. H. Inglesby / A. Ruffner	E. W. Hughes	E. A. Snowden / E L. Sutton	J. I. Hurt
1887 8	V. W. Harrison	J. I. Hurt / W. T. Thayer, Jr.	H. B. Buckner	D. Martin	O. K. Andrews.
1888-90 *	F. C. von Rosenberg	G. S. Vickery	C. B. Burke	D. Martin	A. J. Price
1891 2	F. D. Daniel	H. J. Coffroth	W. B. Tennant	H. M. Martin	W. D. Wall, Jr. / A. G. Joly
1892 4	C. B. Burke	J. H. Covington	F, K, Farr	H, M, Martin	S. W. Martin.
1894 6	J. H. Covington	J. C. Travis	G. H. Powell	H, M Martin	S. W. Martin.
1896 8	J. C. ...	W. W. Ballard	G. H. Powell	H. M. Martin	S, W, Martin.
1898 190	G. H. Powell	C. Richardson	J. W. Davis.	H. M. Martin	S. W. Martin.
1900 02	D. F. Hoy	C. Richardson	J. R. Nal	H. M. Martin	S W. Martin
1902 04	M. Sands	C. Richardson	J R. Nal	H. M. Martin	S. W. Martin.
1904 06	M. Sands	C. Richardson	J. R. Nal	H. M. Martin	S. W. Martin.
96	F. K. Farr	J. R. Neal	J. S. Ferguson	H. M. Martin	S. W. Martin.

* This Conclave met Dec. 31, 1890—Jan. 2, 1891

For purposes of administration, the Fraternity is divided into
fourteen Districts. The geographical limits of these are shown
on accompanying maps. At the head of each is a District Grand
Master. He personally oversees the Chapters, resulting in the
complete unification and understanding among them, and keeping the work of each individual Chapter up to the standard.
He is also expected to know, and to keep in touch with every
alumnus residing in his District.

While the greater part of the government is delegated to the

THE "CHICAGO SPECIAL" EN ROUTE TO A GRAND CONCLAVE

Supreme Executive Committee, still the ultimate and highest
authority in the Fraternity is the Grand Conclave. The Conclaves' legislation in the past has been intended to hamper as
little as possible the powers of the S. E. C. Conclaves have been
held as follows: Baltimore, Md., 1876; Richmond, Va., 1878;
Abingdon, Va., 1880; Knoxville, Tenn., 1883; Lynchburg, Va.,
1885; Nashville, Tenn., 1887; Atlanta, Ga., 1888; Baltimore, Md.,
1890; Washington, D. C., 1892; Richmond, Va., 1894; Indianapolis, Ind., 1896; Chattanooga, Tenn., 1898; Philadelphia, Pa.,

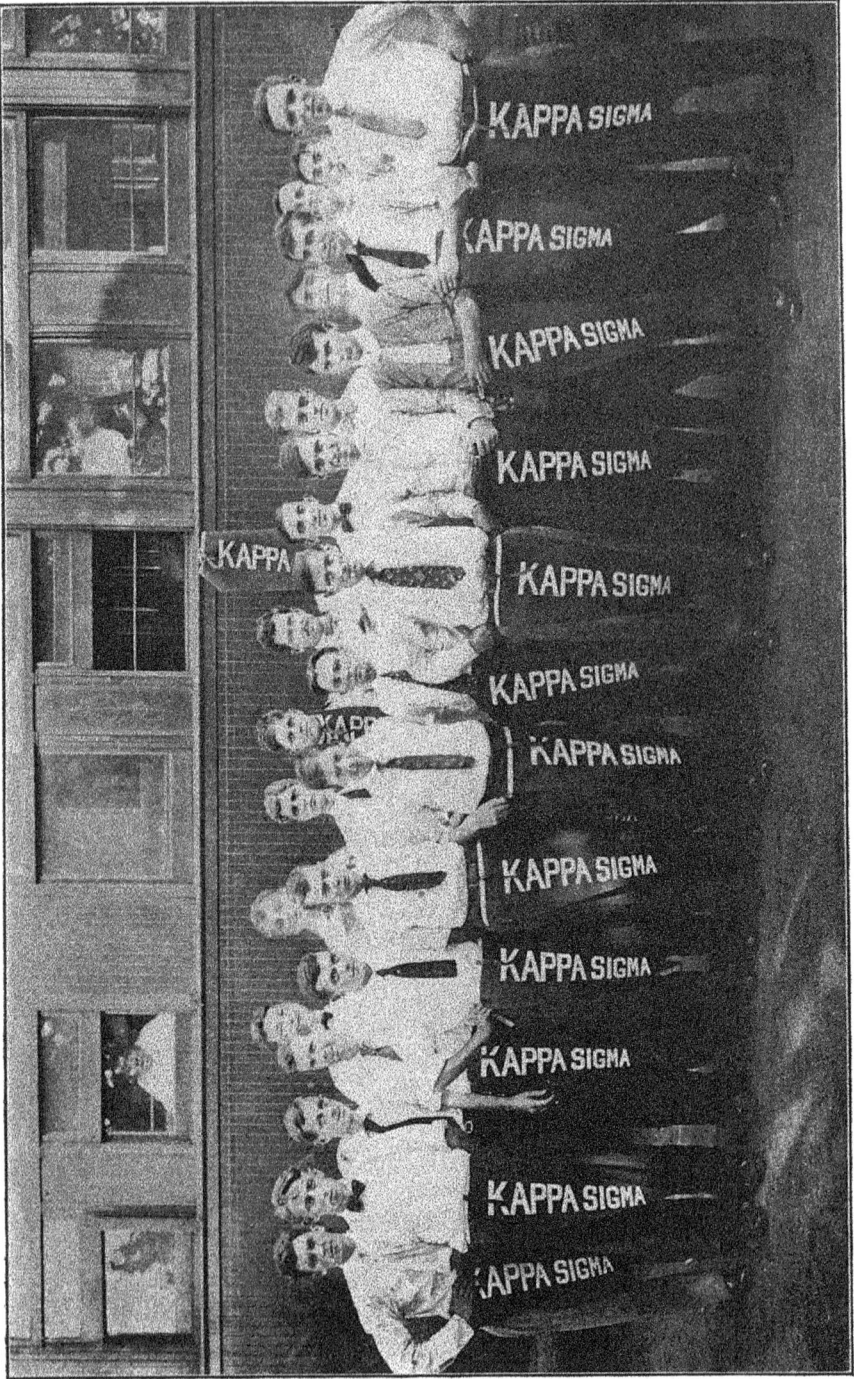

NEW YORK ALUMNI EN ROUTE TO A GRAND CONCLAVE

1900; New Orleans, La., 1902; St. Louis, Mo., 1904; Lookout Mountain, Tenn., 1906. These meetings are usually held at some popular hotel or resort. They have grown into large concourses with hundreds of the silver-grays and undergraduates, with their wives and sweethearts, arriving on special trains and cars from all over the country. The St. Louis (1904) Conclave during the World's Fair was one of the largest meetings of Greek letter

KAPPA SIGMA HOUSE, CHICAGO
The G. M's Room
Library
Freshmen at Work

men ever assembled. The last (1906) Conclave was held at Lookout Mountain, Tenn., and the next (1908) Conclave will probably be held at Put-in-Bay, Ohio. Detailed accounts and minutes of all the Conclaves may be found in the *Caduceus,* the *Star and Crescent,* and various printed reports.

There are also District Conclaves, usually held annually in each District. They are informal gatherings for fraternal intercourse

KAPPA SIGMA'S ASSEMBLED AT A DISTRICT CONCLAVE

and for general discussion of anything of importance, but not

ARMS OF THE FRATERNITY.—At the last moment it was found
advisable to hold back the coat-of-arms from the engraver,
pending the adoption of certain suggestions for its perfection
in correctness and adaptability.   Purchasers of this book will
be supplied with the official design when engraved.

MAY, 1907.

THE "FIVE O'CLOCK CLUB" AT A GRAND CONCLAVE

tive arms.   The colors of the Fraternity are scarlet, white and
emerald green.   The Fraternity flower is the lily-of-the-valley.
No other fraternity pays more attention to visitation of alumni
chapters, for a feature of the organization of which much is made
consists in keeping the alumni in touch with one another.   This
visiting is done principally by members of the S. E. C. and D.
G. M's.   The number of alumni meetings in Kappa Sigma is
frequently remarked.

KAPPA SIGMA'S ASSEMBLED AT A DISTRICT CONCI

and for general discussion of anything of importance, but not for legislation.   Many of the alumni, and the undergraduates for the most part *en masse,* attend them, and although not an old institution in the Fraternity, they have been successful.

The arms of the Fraternity, displayed in the frontispiece, are: Gules and vert, on a chevron argent five estoiles of the first. Crest: on a wreath of its colors a dexter cubit arm proper holding a caduceus erect or.   Individual Chapters may adopt distinc-

THE "FIVE O'CLOCK CLUB" AT A GRAND CONCLAVE

tive arms.   The colors of the Fraternity are scarlet, white and emerald green.   The Fraternity flower is the lily-of-the-valley.

No other fraternity pays more attention to visitation of alumni chapters, for a feature of the organization of which much is made consists in keeping the alumni in touch with one another.   This visiting is done principally by members of the S. E. C. and D. G. M's.   The number of alumni meetings in Kappa Sigma is frequently remarked.

KAPPA SIGMA HOUSE, IOWA

HOMES OF KAPPA SIGMA

The Fraternity has always insisted upon chapter houses when possible. In 1870, the house occupied at the University of Virginia was one of the first fraternity houses in the country and the first fraternity house in the South. In 1882, the house occupied by the Chapter at the University of the South was among the first houses owned and occupied in that section. In 1883, at the Knoxville Conclave, Kappa Sigma made .the first attempt to control the building of houses, by the national organization of a fraternity. This was a failure, and it has since been the policy to place responsibility on the individual Chapters. In 1895, Kappa Sigma erected a house at Maine, the Fraternity's first Northern chapter house to be owned and the first fraternity house in the state of Maine. The three fraternities now having the largest number of homes are Beta Theta Pi, Phi Delta Theta, and Kappa Sigma.

It is but a matter of time before all Chapters, where there are no restrictions by college authorities, even if houses are not the vogue, will be compelled by their general organizations to possess a home. At present there are Kappa Sigma houses at the following institutions: Maine, Bowdoin, New Hampshire, Massachusetts State, Harvard, Cornell, Syracuse, Pennsylvania State, Pennsylvania, Lehigh, Maryland, George Washington, William and Mary, Wofford, Vanderbilt, University of the South, Ohio State, Case, Washington and Jefferson, Michigan, Purdue, Indiana, Illinois, Lake Forest, Chicago, Wisconsin, Minnesota, Iowa, Nebraska, William Jewell, Missouri State, Missouri Mines, Baker, Arkansas, Oklahoma, Millsaps, Louisiana State, Texas, Colorado, Colorado Mines, Stanford, California, Washington,

Oregon, Idaho. Some Chapters occupy whole sections of college dormitories.

Some of the houses are noted in the fraternity world. That at one Eastern institution has been described as "the best planned at Cornell"; that at Texas, "the best house owned in the South"; that at Iowa, "the most elegant house in the Middle West"; that at Stanford "the finest house on the Pacific Coast." Some of them have been historic. One recently occupied by the Maryland Chapter was the Baltimore home of General Robert E. Lee. The one now occupied at Missouri Mines was the headquarters of the

KAPPA SIGMA HOUSE, CORNELL

Army of the Missouri during the civil war. The Harvard house at Cambridge, Mass., and the William and Mary at Williamsburg, the ancient capital of Virginia, both stand on historic ground. At the California and Colorado houses, in the midst of the two American playgrounds, many alumni visit, making these Kappa Sigma seats their headquarters. More or less all the houses in the large centers are on many occasions utilized for this purpose. The Virginia Chapter and the remainder of the Fraternity have collected funds for a house for the mother Chapter as a memorial, to be known as "McCormick Hall."

KAPPA SIGMA HOUSE, LEHIGH

VOL. XXI.   OCTOBER 20, 1906   NO. 1

The Caduceus
of
Kappa Sigma

SEMPER

Published
by

the
Fraternity

THE PUBLICATIONS

The publications of the Fraternity are extensive. From the little pamphlet struck off on a press of the Virginia Polytechnic Institute by Dr. C. E. Wingo and William Freneau Page, they have grown to the point where the periodical literature alone is over a thousand pages annually, probably a larger amount than of any other fraternity. Believing that a wide acquaintance among its members is one of its sources of strength, the organization fosters all efforts of this kind. The most important publication of any Greek letter society is its magazine; in the case of Kappa Sigma known as *The Caduceus.*

Previous to 1878, there had been several spasmodic attempts by various fraternities to found magazines, but with two exceptions, these were unsuccessful and but a few numbers were issued. The period from 1878 to 1885 saw productions of this kind placed on a sound basis, although most of those established by the New England fraternities have since failed. At first, it was argued that Kappa Sigma was of too secret a nature for an open publication. However, the Lynchburg Conclave of 1885 authorized the issuance of the *Kappa Sigma Quarterly.* Brought up in the cultivated and literary home of his father, General Terry of the Confederacy, Frank Hanson Terry, now a newspaper man of Wytheville, Va., was elected the first editor. In 1887, Ed. L. Sutton, now managing editor of the Semi-Weekly *Atlanta Journal,* became editor, and continued as such till the Baltimore Conclave of 1890. This convention made the magazine a bi-monthly, and changed its name to *The Star and Crescent,* rechristened before issue *The Caduceus of Kappa Sigma.* During 1891, Duncan Martin, now of the Memphis bar, was editor. From 1892 to 1895,

8

the brilliant but erring George William Warner was editor. J. Harry Covington, of the Maryland bar, was editor from 1895 to 1905. During 1905 and until June, 1906, Professor Finis King Farr, of Cumberland, was in charge. The last and present editor is Guy T. Viskniskki, of the McClure News Syndicate.

The *Caduceus* is now in its twenty-first volume. It has never less than 176 pages in each of its five issues for the year. At least forty pages are given to alumni notes. Due notice is taken

KAPPA SIGMA HOUSE, IDAHO

of all important college and fraternity matters, the interests of Kappa Sigma receiving the most attention. Illustrations are abundantly used, the five numbers of 1905-1906 containing two hundred and forty half-tones. It has been pronounced the peer of any magazine ever issued from the Greek press. It is also among those claiming the honor of the largest circulation.

The first Catalogue of the Fraternity was prepared in 1881 by S. A. Jackson. Another edition by Brother Jackson appeared in 1886. In 1897 was published a Directory of Kappa Sigma, by

George Vaughan, now of the Arkansas bar. For a number of
years a history and catalogue, complete in every detail, was in
course of collection by this gentleman. Had this catalogue been
published, it would have been in some respects one of the most
complete ever issued by a college fraternity. Kappa Sigma began
at a very early date after her origin to collect the "college honors"
of her membership, which honors are lacking for early members

KAPPA SIGMA HOUSE, TEXAS

in most fraternity catalogues. All of these records were completely destroyed by fire at Little Rock, Ark. The accident was
peculiarly unfortunate. In 1904 a pocket Address Book was published under the direction of David F. Hoy, registrar of Cornell
University and now Catalogue Editor of the Fraternity.

In 1906 Brother Hoy issued a second and enlarged edition of
the Address Book. He has collected complete data for another

catalogue, which will contain some new features in fraternity cataloguing, and which will be published at the will of the Supreme Executive Committee.

The blanks for this catalogue contained the following questions: Full name without initials; Chapter; permanent address; occupation; date of initiation; date of birth; place of birth; full name and address of father; full maiden name and

KAPPA SIGMA HOUSE, SYRACUSE

address of mother; full maiden name of wife; full name and address of wife's father; date and place of marriage; full names in order of birth and addresses of all children; names of preparatory schools and dates of attendance; names of colleges and dates of attendance; degrees received—colleges and dates; membership in college fraternities and societies; college honors, prizes, scholarships, athletics, etc.; membership in learned, fraternal, and other non-college societies; list of books and articles published;

political positions and places of trust which have been held; reference to any publication containing biographical or genealogical information; names and addresses of all Kappa Sigma relatives; name and address of personal friend who will always know address; remarks; signature; business address; temporary address; residence address; date of information.

Other printed literature is becoming so extensive it is difficult

KAPPA SIGMA HOUSE, ARKANSAS

to keep up with it. The Fraternity, like four others, issues a secret bulletin in addition to its regular magazine. This is *The Star and Crescent*, which appears quarterly. It contains reports of officers, and other official communications to the Fraternity, items of fraternity news of such a nature that their publication in *The Caduceus* would be improper, and in general all such things as concern the inner workings of the Fraternity. A unique publication is *The Secret Book of Kappa Sigma*. It gives, from a Kappa Sigma standpoint, of course, the "standing" or "rating" of all fraternities and of the chapters of each fraternity in Kappa Sigma colleges. Reports of Chapters and circular reports of various offices of the Fraternity are voluminous. The *Yellow Journal* is issued from the office of the Worthy Grand Master, and circulates only among the national officers. All Chapters are required at least annually, to send out a letter to their alumni, most of these letters being printed. The Boston Alumni have published an address book of the alumni of New England. There are other locality directories published under

KAPPA SIGMA HOUSE, NEBRASKA

different auspices for states and cities. The Cumberland, Maine, North Georgia, Maryland Military and Naval, Wofford and Massachusetts Chapters have issued annuals. The Chapters at the University of the South, Centenary, and Vermont have written histories. The Illinois, Swarthmore, Wabash, Purdue and Massachusetts Chapters have issued catalogues. The general Fraternity has had printed Kappa Sigma calendars. In 1896 the Bowdoin Chapter issued a small songbook. A songbook was published by the Fraternity in 1902. Another is in process of collection. There are a number of pamphlets containing Kappa Sigma songs and poems. There are three editions of the ritual and five editions of the Constitution. Many reports of Conclaves have been printed under separate covers.

Kappa Sigma has been very fortunate in the preservation of its history. This has been chiefly due to the fact that it was but twelve years between the time the third Chapter was established, the records of the second Chapter having been lost, and the appearance of the Fraternity's magazine. Also the early documents,

KAPPA SIGMA HOUSE, WASHINGTON AND JEFFERSON

so frequently missing in many fraternities, were all collected and preserved at an early date. The events in the Fraternity's history, previous to the existence of the magazine, which have not been covered by historical articles in the *Quarterly, Caduceus, Star and Crescent,* and catalogues, are preserved in the recently published *Early Letters and Papers of Kappa Sigma,* compiled by Boutwell Dunlap, now historian of the Fraternity. Freshmen are examined upon the Fraternity's history.

KAPPA SIGMA HOUSE, BOWDOIN

OTHER FRATERNITIES

Some years ago it was customary to classify fraternities on a basis of their origin, into Eastern or Northern, Southern and Western. They are now usually classified as either national or sectional. "The national fraternities include those generally represented in all sections of the country. Of these Beta Theta Pi, Phi Delta Theta, Sigma Alpha Epsilon, Sigma Chi, Kappa Sigma, Phi Kappa Psi, and Phi Gamma Delta are prominent types. The sectional fraternities are Eastern and Southern. The Eastern group consists of Alpha Delta Phi, Delta Phi Theta, Delta Chi, Sigma Phi, Psi Upsilon, Kappa Alpha (Northern) and Delta Psi. The Southern group includes Kappa Alpha (Southern order), and Pi Kappa Alpha. Delta Kappa Epsilon and Chi Psi, originating in the Eastern States, have what might be termed a limited national development. Alpha Tau Omega, Kappa Sigma, Sigma Nu and Sigma Alpha Epsilon, originally distinctively Southern, have completely lost that character. Zeta Psi and Chi Psi are difficult to classify." (Baird's *Manual of American College Fraternities,* Sixth edition.) The sectional fraternities were once more important than they now are. In most cases they have few petitions for charters and seldom establish new chapters. They have failed to take advantage of the larger new institutions, maintaining many chapters in unimportant colleges. Their conventions are attended by a small number of members. Lacking in alumni clubs, they hold but few meetings in the large centers, and these seldom attract any attention. The fraternities are not a living reality to their alumni and the alumnus' active connection is soon lost. Their literature is confined to catalogues, which quickly grow out of date, and they publish no magazines. The funds and membership are not sufficient to carry on the enterprises of the national orders. As fraternities they attract little attention. Collegians prefer the national fraternities, says a recent writer of authority upon the subject.

The parent stem of the Greek letter college fraternity was Phi Beta Kappa, established at William and Mary in 1776.[6] It was extended to Yale (1780), Harvard (1781), Dartmouth (1787), and Union (1817). Modeled after Phi Beta Kappa was

KAPPA SIGMA HOUSE, WOFFORD

the Kappa Alpha Society, the first Greek letter society in the present sense of the word, founded in 1825, to which ascent can be traced all the American college fraternities. Owing to the anti-Masonic outbreak in 1831, upon the advice of John Quincy Adams, Edward Everett, and others, the secrets of Phi Beta

[6] The best account of the origin of Phi Beta Kappa may be found in "The Original Records of the Phi Beta Kappa Society, 1776-1781," by L. G. Tyler, K. S., *William and Mary Quarterly Historical Magazine*, April, 1896.

CALIFORNIA

Kappa were made public, since which time it has been an honorary organization.

The general men's fraternities are:[7]

Alpha Chi Rho. Founded at Trinity College, Hartford, Conn., in 1895. Chapters, 7; active, 6; inactive, 1. Number of initiates, 258. Publishes the *Garnet and White.* No catalogue.

Alpha Delta Phi. Founded at Hamilton College, Clinton, N. Y., in 1832. Chapters, 31; active, 24; inactive, 7. Number of

KAPPA SIGMA HOUSE, COLORADO COLLEGE

initiates, 9,406. Publishes no magazine. Last catalogue in 1899.

Alpha Tau Omega. Founded at Virginia Military Institute, Lexington, Va., in 1865. Chapters, 82; active, 51; inactive, 31. Number of initiates, 6,486. Publishes the *Palm.* Last catalogue in 1903.

Beta Theta Pi. Founded at Miami University, Oxford, Ohio,

---

[7] These statistics are taken from the sixth (1905) edition of *Baird's Manual of American College Fraternities.*

in 1839. Chapters, 88; active, 67; inactive, 21. Number of initiates, 14,046. Publishes the *Beta Theta Pi*. Last catalogue in 1899.

Chi Phi. Resulted from a union in 1874 of the Northern Order of Chi Phi and the Southern Order of Chi Phi. The Northern order of Chi Phi, resulted from the union in 1867 of Chi Phi, founded at Princeton University, Princeton, N. J., in 1854, with Chi Phi, founded at Hobart College, Geneva, N. Y., in 1860. The Southern Order of Chi Phi was founded at

KAPPA SIGMA HOUSE, MAINE

the University of North Carolina, Chapel Hill, N. C., in 1858. Chapters, 46; active, 20; inactive, 26. Number of initiates, 4,422. No magazine. Last catalogue in 1890.

Chi Psi. Founded at Union College, Schenectady, N. Y., in 1841. Chapters, 29; active, 18; inactive, 11. Number of initiates, 4,459. Publishes a sub-rosa magazine, the *Purple and Gold*. Last catalogue in 1902.

Delta Kappa Epsilon. Founded at Yale College, New Haven, Conn., in 1844. Chapters, 54; active, 41; inactive, 13. Number of initiates, 15,000. Publishes the *Delta Kappa Epsilon Quarterly*. Last catalogue in 1900.

Delta Phi. Founded at Union College, Schenectady, N. Y., in 1827. Chapters, 16; active, 11; inactive, 5. Number of initiates, 3,341.. No magazine. Last catalogue in 1897.

Delta Psi. Founded at Columbia College, New York City, in 1847. Chapters, 19; active, 8; inactive, 11. Number of initiates, 2,989. No magazine. Last catalogue in 1898.

Delta Tau Delta. Founded at Bethany College, Bethany, W. Va., in 1859. Chapters, 75; active, 47; inactive, 28. Number of

KAPPA SIGMA HOUSE, NEW HAMPSHIRE

initiates, 7,486. Publishes the *Rainbow.* Last catalogue in 1897 (with supplement in 1902).

Delta Upsilon (Non-secret). Founded at Williams College, Williamstown, Mass., in 1834 (or as claimed by some authorities, founded at Troy, N. Y., in 1847). Chapters, 41; active, 36; inactive, 5. Number of initiates, 9,169. Publishes the *Delta Upsilon Quarterly.* Last catalogue in 1903.

Kappa Alpha (Northern). Founded at Union College, Schenectady, N. Y., in 1825. Chapters, 9; active, 7; inactive, 2. Number of initiates, 1,666. No magazine. Last catalogue in 1902.

Kappa Alpha (Southern). Founded at Washington and Lee

University, Lexington, Va., in 1865. Chapters, 60; active, 49; inactive, 11. Number of initiates, 6,146. Publishes the *Kappa Alpha Journal*. Last catalogue in 1901.

Kappa Sigma. Founded at the University of Virginia, Charlottesville, Va., in 1869. Chapters, 91; active, 76; inactive, 15. Number of initiates, 7155 (statistics of 1906). Publishes the *Caduceus* and the secret *Star and Crescent.* Last catalogue in 1906.

Phi Delta Theta. Founded at Miami University, Oxford, Ohio, itiates, 13,161. Publishes the *Scroll of Phi Delta Theta* and the secret *Palladium.* Last catalogue in 1907.

Phi Gamma Delta. Founded at Jefferson College, Canonsburg, Pa., in 1848. Chapters, 81; active, 57; inactive, 24. Number of in 1848. Chapters, 95; active, 69; inactive, 26. Number of ininitiates, 9,979. Publishes the *Phi Gamma Delta.* Last catalogue in 1898.

Phi Kappa Psi. Founded at Jefferson College, Canonsburg, Pa., in 1852. Chapters, 63; active, 42; inactive, 21. Number of initiates, 9,806. Publishes the *Shield.* Last catalogue in 1902.

Phi Kappa Sigma. Founded at the University of Pennsylvania, Philadelphia, Pa., in 1850. Chapters, 41; active, 24; inactive, 17. Number of initiates, 3,122. Publishes the sub-rosa *Phi Kappa Sigma News Letter.* Last catalogue in 1905.

Phi Sigma Kappa. Founded at Massachusetts State College, Amherst, Mass., in 1873. Chapters, 19; active, 19; inactive, 0; Number of initiates, 1,551. Publishes the sub-rosa *Signet.* Last catalogue in 1902.

Pi Kappa Alpha. Founded at the University of Virginia, Charlottesville, Va., in 1868. Chapters, 33; active, 29; inactive, 4. Number of initiates, 2,427. Publishes the *Shield and Diamond* and the secret *Dagger and Key.* Last catalogue in 1891.

Psi Upsilon. Founded at Union College, Schenectady, N. Y., in 1833. Chapters, 23; active, 22; inactive, 1. Number of initiates, 10,428. No magazine. Last catalogue in 1902.

Sigma Alpha Epsilon. Founded at the University of Alabama, University, Ala., in 1856. Chapters, 94; active, 66; inactive, 28. Number of initiates, 9,383. Publishes the *Record* and the secret *Phi Alpha.* Last catalogue in 1904.

Sigma Chi. Founded at Miami University, Oxford, Ohio, in 1855. Chapters, 76; active, 53; inactive, 23. Number of initiates, 8,358. Publishes the *Sigma Chi Quarterly* and the secret *Bulletin.* Last catalogue in 1902.

Sigma Nu. Founded at the Virginia Military Institute, Lexington, Va., in 1869. Chapters, 69; active, 54; inactive, 15. Number of initiates, 5,357. Publishes the *Delta.* Last catalogue in 1902.

Sigma Phi. Founded at Union College, Schenectady, N. Y., in 1827. Chapters, 10; active, 8; inactive, 2. Number of initiates, 2,685. No magazine. Last catalogue in 1892.

Sigma Phi Epsilon. Founded at Richmond College, Richmond, Va., in 1901. Chapters, 14; active, 13; inactive, 1. Number of initiates, 248. Publishes the *Sigma Phi Epsilon Journal.* No catalogue.

Theta Chi. Founded at Norwich University, Northfield, Vt., in 1856. Chapters, 2; active, 2; inactive, 0. Number of initiates, 341. No magazine. No catalogue.

Theta Delta Chi. Founded at Union College, Schenectady, N. Y., in 1848. Chapters, 41; active, 24; inactive, 17. Number of initiates, 5,141. Publishes the *Shield.* Last catalogue in 1901.

Zeta Psi. Founded at the University of the City of New York, New York City, in 1847. Chapters, 32; active, 22; inactive, 10. Number of initiates, 5,924. Last catalogue in 1899.

The general sororities for women, with college and date of foundation, are Alpha Chi Omega (De Pauw, 1885), Alpha Omicron Pi (Barnard, 1897), Alpha Phi (Syracuse, 1872), Alpha Xi Delta (Lombard, 1902), Beta Sigma Omicron (Missouri, 1888), Chi Omega (Arkansas, 1895), Delta Delta Delta (Boston, 1888), Delta Gamma (Mississippi, 1872), Delta Sigma (Tufts, 1895), Gamma Phi Beta (Syracuse, 1874), Kappa Alpha Theta (De Pauw, 1870), Kappa Delta (Virginia State Female Normal, 1897), Kappa Kappa Gamma (Monmouth, 1870), Pi Beta Phi (Monmouth, 1867), Sigma Kappa (Colby, 1874), Sigma Sigma Sigma (Virginia State Normal, 1898), Zeta Tau Alpha (Virginia State Normal, 1898).

The professional fraternities, with college and date of foundation are: Alpha Chi Gamma (women-musical), Ottawa, Ohio,

1899; Alpha Epsilon Iota (women-medical), Michigan, 1890; Alpha Kappa Kappa (medical-regular), Dartmouth, 1888; Alpha Kappa Phi (law), Northwestern, 1902; Alpha Mu Pi Omega (medical-regular), Pennsylvania, 1891; Alpha Omega Delta (medical-regular), Buffalo, 1879; Alpha Zeta (agricultural-technical), Ohio State, 1897; Beta Mu Delta (biology), Syracuse. 1903; Beta Phi Sigma (pharmacy), Buffalo, 1889; Chi Zeta Chi (medical-regular), Georgia, 1903; Delta Chi (law), Cornell, 1890; Delta Sigma Delta (dental), Michigan, 1883; Epsilon Tau (women-homeopathic), Boston, 1896; Eta Pi Alpha (theological), St. Lawrence, 1891; Gamma Eta Alpha (law, Maine, 1901; Kappa Delta Epsilon (women-musical), Allegheny, 1899; Nu Sigma Nu (medical-regular), Michigan, 1882; Omega Psi (women-medical), Northwestern, 1894; Omega Upsilon Phi (medical-regular), Buffalo, 1895; Phi Alpha Delta (law), Kent college of law, 1897; Phi Alpha Gamma (medical-homeopathic), New York Homeopathic Medical College, 1894; Phi Alpha Sigma (medical-regular), Bellevue, 1886; Phi Beta Pi (medical-regular) West Pennsylvania Medical College, 1891; Phi Chi (pharmacy), Michigan, 1883; Phi Chi (medical-regular), Vermont, 1886, and Louisville Medical College, 1894; Phi Delta (medical-regular), Long Island Hospital Medical College, 1901; Phi Delta Phi (law), Michigan, 1869; Phi Mu Epsilon (women-musical), De Pauw, 1892; Phi Rho Sigma (medical-regular), Northwestern, 1890; Pi Lambda Sigma (women-library economy), Syracuse, 1903; Pi Mu (medical-regular), Virginia, 1892; Psi Omega (dental), Baltimore College of Dental Surgery, 1892; Q. T. V. (agricultural-scientific), Massachusetts State College, 1869; Sigma Alpha Iota (women-musical), Michigan, 1903; Sigma Rho Alpha (architecture), Syracuse, 1902; Theta Lambda Phi (law), Dickenson, 1903; Theta Xi (engineering-scientific), Rensselaer Polytechnic, 1864; Xi Psi Phi (dental), Michigan, 1889; Zeta Phi (women-medical), Syracuse, 1900.

The inactive general fraternities, with college and date of foundation, are: Alpha Gamma (Cumberland, 1867), Alpha Kappa Phi (Center, 1858), Alpha Sigma Chi (Rutgers and Cornell, 1871), Delta Beta Phi (Cornell, 1878), Delta Epsilon (Roanoke, 1862), Iota Alpha Kappa (Union, 1858), Kappa Alpha

(North Carolina, 1859), Kappa Phi Lambda (Jefferson, 1862), Kappa Sigma Kappa (Virginia Military Institute, 1867), Mystical Seven (Wesleyan, 1837), Mu Pi Lambda (Washington and Lee, 1895), Phi Alpha (College of City of New York, 1878), Phi Alpha Chi (Randolph-Macon, 1883), Phi Kappa Alpha (Brown, 1870), Phi Phi Phi (Austin, 1894), Pi Kappa Tau (Iowa, 1895), Phi Delta Kappa (Washington and Jefferson, 1874), Phi Mu Omicron (South Carolina, 1858), Phi Sigma (Lombard, 1857), Psi Theta Psi (Washington and Lee, 1885), Sigma Alpha (Roanoke, 1859), Sigma Alpha Theta, Sigma Delta Pi (Dartmouth, 1858), Upsilon Beta (Pennsylvania College, 1863), W. W. W. or Rainbow (Mississippi, 1849), Zeta Phi (Missouri, 1870).

Although not in all respects satisfactory, the best general sketch of fraternities is the sixth edition of William Raimond Baird's *American College Fraternities*. The following fraternities have published manuals or histories: Psi Upsilon, Phi Delta Theta, Beta Theta Pi, Theta Delta Chi, Phi Kappa Psi, Sigma Alpha Epsilon, and Kappa Sigma. There is historical matter, principally devoted to chapter histories and ranging from a paragraph to several pages on a chapter, in the catalogues of Alpha Delta Phi, Chi Phi, Chi Psi, Delta Upsilon, Kappa Alpha (Northern Order), Kappa Alpha (Southern Order), Kappa Sigma, Phi Kappa Sigma, Sigma Alpha Epsilon, Sigma Chi, Sigma Nu, Sigma Phi and Zeta Psi. Other important historical sources are the magazines—published by Alpha Tau Omega, Beta Theta Pi, Delta Kappa Epsilon, Delta Tau Delta, Delta Upsilon, Kappa Alpha (Southern Order), Kappa Sigma, Phi Delta Theta, Phi Gamma Delta, Phi Kappa Psi, Pi Kappa Alpha, Sigma Alpha Epsilon, Sigma Chi, Sigma Nu, and Theta Delta Chi. The best defense of fraternities is a collection of views upon the subject by forty-eight college presidents under the title, *The American College Fraternity*, edited by W. A. Crawford, K. S. The most complete bibliography of fraternities is contained in W. B. Palmer's *History of Phi Delta Theta*.

Familiar tongues that faintly call,
    Remembered songs of days gone by,
Dim echoes, they too softly fall
    On ears that hunger for reply;
For memory wakes and love makes cry
    In tones of greeting and of praise,
"To you I drain the health-cup dry,
    Old comrades of my college days."

Whate'er your emblems, hail to all!
    Because ye loved them so shall I;
'Tis sweet each old friend to recall;
    The Shield and Diamond, Sigma Chi,
D. U., Phi Gam, and every Phi
    I loved; ye, Theta Delts, K. A's,
And Dekes—greeting to all I cry,
    Old comrades of my college days.

Good cheer and blessing to ye all,
    Old friends of days that shall not die:
Like sunbeams dancing on the wall
    May all the happy moments fly.
Companions still, may ye and I,
    Though straying far on several ways,
Remember well the days gone by,
    Old comrades of my college days.

L'ENVOI.

But, Brothers, as the seasons fly,
    While bright the Star and Crescent blaze,
Still closer grows our nearer tie,
    Old comrades of my college days.

                                James S. Wilson (Nu).

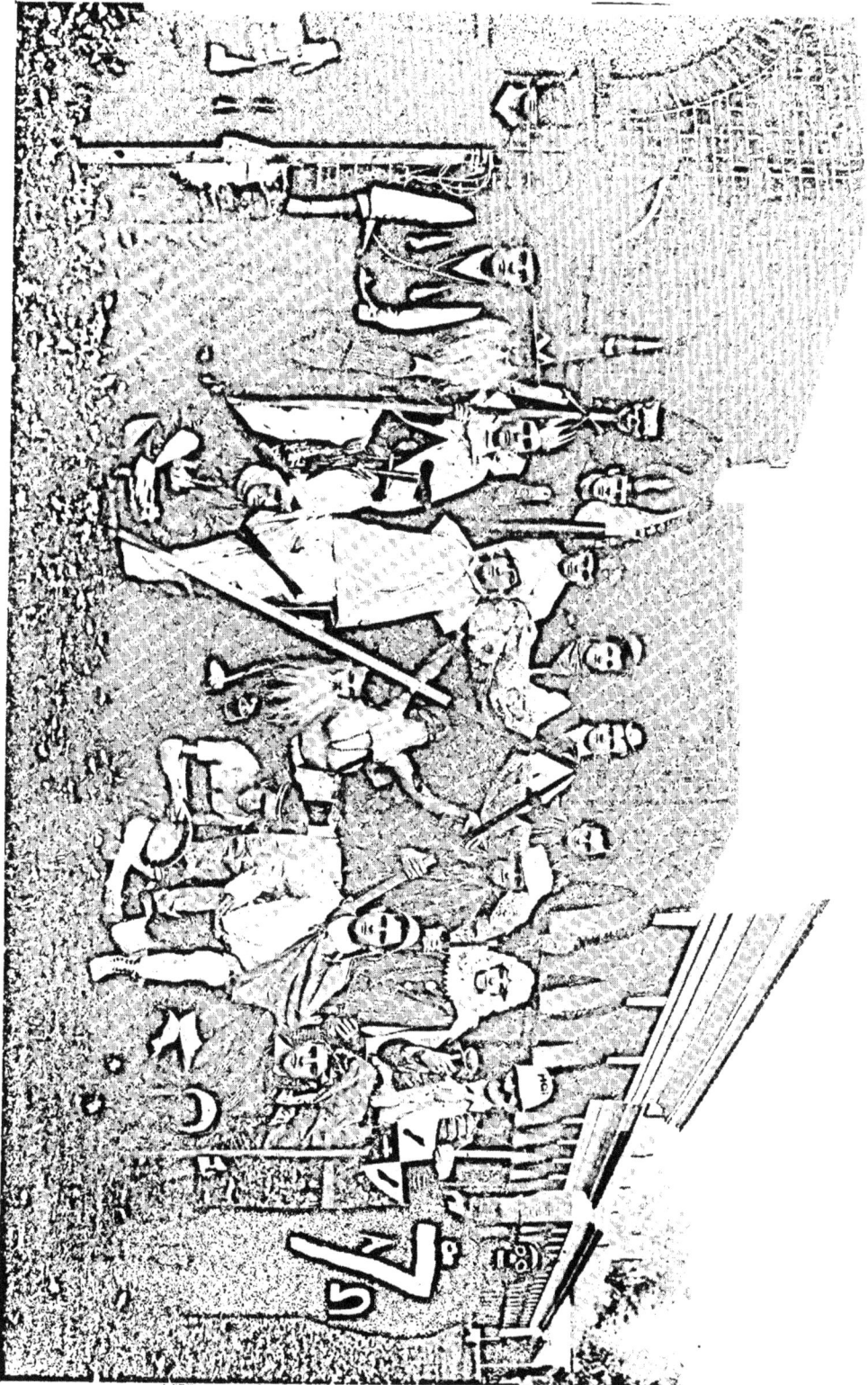

PARTICIPANTS IN THE CORONATION OF THE KING OF THE HOT FEET', VIRGINIA

APPENDIX A

FRATERNITIES IN KAPPA SIGMA COLLEGES

Alabama Polytechnic Institute, Auburn, Ala.—Sigma Alpha Epsilon, 1878; Phi Delta Theta, 1879; Alpha Tau Omega, 1879; Kappa Alpha, 1883; Sigma Nu, 1890; Pi Kappa Alpha, 1895; Kappa Sigma, 1900.

Alabama, University of, University, Ala.—Delta Kappa Epsilon, 1847; Alpha Delta Phi, 1851-58; Phi Gamma Delta, 1855; Sigma Alpha Epsilon, 1856; Kappa Sigma, 1871; Sigma Nu, 1874; Sigma Chi, 1876-77; Phi Delta Theta, 1877; Alpha Tau Omega, 1885; Kappa Alpha, 1885; Phi Kappa Sigma, 1903.

Arkansas, University of, Fayetteville, Ark.—Alpha Tau Omega, 1882-82; Kappa Sigma, 1890; Sigma Alpha Epsilon, 1894; Kappa Alpha, 1895; Sigma Nu, 1904; Pi Kappa Alpha, 1904; Sigma Chi, 1905.

Baker University, Baldwin, Kan.—Phi Gamma Delta, 1865-68; Kappa Sigma, 1903; Delta Tau Delta, 1903.

Bowdoin College, Brunswick, Me.—Alpha Delta Phi, 1841; Psi Upsilon, 1843; Chi Psi, 1844-46; Delta Kappa Epsilon, 1844; Theta Delta Chi, 1854; Delta Upsilon, 1857; Zeta Psi, 1868; Kappa Sigma, 1895; Beta Theta Pi, 1900.

Brown University, Providence, R. I.—Alpha Delta Phi, 1836; Delta Phi, 1838; Psi Upsilon, 1840; Beta Theta Pi, 1847; Delta Kappa Epsilon, 1850; Delta Psi, 1852-53; Zeta Psi, 1852; Theta Delta Chi, 1853; Chi Psi, 1860-71; Delta Upsilon, 1860; Chi Phi, 1872-95; Phi Delta Theta, 1889; Alpha Tau Omega, 1894; Delta Tau Delta, 1896; Kappa Sigma, 1898; Phi Gamma Delta, 1902; Phi Kappa Psi, 1902; Phi Sigma Kappa, 1906.

Bucknell University, Lewisburg, Pa.—Phi Kappa Psi, 1855; Sigma Chi, 1864; Theta Delta Chi, 1866-73; Phi Gamma Delta, 1882; Sigma Alpha Epsilon, 1893; Kappa Sigma, 1896.

California, University of, Berkeley, Cal.—Zeta Psi, 1870; Phi Delta Theta, 1873; Chi Phi, 1875; Delta Kappa Epsilon, 1876; Beta Theta Pi, 1879; Phi Gamma Delta, 1881; Sigma Chi, 1886;

Sigma Nu, 1892; Chi Psi, 1894; Sigma Alpha Epsilon, 1894; Kappa Alpha, 1895; Delta Upsilon, 1896; Theta Delta Chi, 1900; Phi Kappa Psi, 1900; Alpha Tau Omega, 1900; Kappa Sigma, 1901; Psi Upsilon, 1902; Phi Kappa Sigma, 1903.

Case School of Applied Science, Cleveland, O.—Zeta Psi, 1885; Phi Delta Theta, 1896; Kappa Sigma, 1903; Beta Theta Pi, 1905; Sigma Alpha Epsilon, 1905; Phi Kappa Psi, 1906.

Centenary College, Jackson, La.—Phi Kappa Sigma, 1855-61; Delta Kappa Epsilon, 1857-62; Chi Phi, 1858-61; Kappa Sigma, 1885-04; Kappa Alpha, 1891-04; Pi Kappa Alpha, 1902-04.

Chicago, University of, Chicago, Ill.—Zeta Psi, 1864-87; Phi Kappa Psi, 1865; Phi Delta Theta, 1865; Beta Theta Pi, 1868; Psi Upsilon, 1869; Delta Kappa Epsilon, 1870; Sigma Nu, 1895; Alpha Delta Phi, 1896; Sigma Chi, 1897; Delta Tau Delta, 1898; Chi Psi, 1899; Delta Upsilon, 1901; Phi Gamma Delta, 1902; Sigma Alpha Epsilon, 1903; Kappa Sigma, 1904; Alpha Tau Omega, 1904; Phi Kappa Sigma, 1905; Sigma Phi Epsilon, 1906.

Colorado College, Colorado Springs, Colo.—Kappa Sigma, 1904; Sigma Chi, 1905;

Colorado State School of Mines, Golden, Colo.— Sigma Nu, 1901; Sigma Alpha Epsilon, 1903; Kappa Sigma, 1904.

Cornell University, Ithaca, N. Y.—Chi Phi, 1868; Kappa Alpha, 1868; Chi Psi, 1869; Zeta Psi, 1869; Phi Kappa Psi, 1869; Delta Upsilon, 1869; Alpha Delta Phi, 1869; Delta Kappa Epsilon, 1870; Theta Delta Chi, 1870; Phi Delta Theta, 1872; Beta Theta Pi, 1874; Psi Upsilon, 1876; Alpha Tau Omega, 1887; Phi Gamma Delta, 1888; Phi Sigma Kappa, 1889; Delta Tau Delta, 1890; Sigma Chi, 1890; Sigma Phi, 1890; Delta Phi, 1891; Sigma Alpha Epsilon, 1891; Kappa Sigma, 1892; Sigma Nu, 1901.

Cumberland University, Lebanon, Tenn.—Beta Theta Pi, 1854-99; Delta Kappa Epsilon, 1857-73; Alpha Delta Phi, 1857-61; Delta Psi, 1858-61; Phi Kappa Sigma, 1859-61; Sigma Alpha Epsilon, 1860; Phi Kappa, Psi, 1860-79; Chi Phi, 1861-61; Alpha Tau Omega, 1868-02; Phi Gamma Delta, 1869-78; Sigma Chi, 1872-80; Kappa Sigma, 1887; Pi Kappa Alpha, 1892.

Dartmouth College, Hanover, N. H.—Psi Upsilon, 1842; Alpha Delta Phi, 1846; Delta Kappa Epsilon, 1853; Zeta Psi, 1855-74.

Theta Delta Chi, 1869; Phi Delta Theta, 1884; Beta Theta Pi, 1889; Sigma Chi, 1893; Phi Kappa Psi, 1896; Phi Gamma Delta, 1901; Delta Tau Delta, 1901; Chi Phi, 1902; Kappa Sigma, 1905

Davidson College, Davidson, N. C.—Beta Theta Pi, 1858; Chi Phi, 1859-69; Pi Kappa Alpha, 1869; Kappa Alpha, 1880; Sigma Alpha Epsilon, 1883; Kappa Sigma, 1890.

Denver, University of, Denver, Colo.—Beta Theta Pi, 1888; Sigma Alpha Epsilon, 1891; Kappa Sigma, 1902.

Dickinson College, Carlisle, Pa.—Zeta Psi, 1853-55; Phi Kappa Sigma, 1854; Phi Kappa Psi, 1859; Sigma Chi, 1859; Theta Delta Chi, 1861-96; Chi Phi, 1869-92; Beta Theta Pi, 1874; Phi Delta Theta, 1880; Sigma Alpha Epsilon, 1890; Kappa Sigma, 1902, Alpha Chi Rho, 1905.

Emory College, Oxford, Ga.—Kappa Alpha, 1869; Chi Phi, 1869; Phi Delta Theta, 1871; Alpha Tau Omega, 1881; Sigma Alpha Epsilon, 1881; Delta Tau Delta, 1882; Sigma Nu, 1884; Kappa Sigma, 1887-91.

Emory and Henry College, Emory, Va.—Phi Kappa Sigma, 1856-61; Kappa Sigma, 1873-95; Sigma Alpha Epsilon, 1884-95; Kappa Alpha, 1893-95.

George Washington University (until 1904 known as *Columbian University*), Washington, D. C.—Sigma Alpha Epsilon, 1858; Sigma Chi, 1864; Phi Kappa Psi, 1868-99; Alpha Tau Omega, 1874-88; Kappa Sigma, 1892; Kappa Alpha, 1894; Phi Sigma Kappa, 1899; Delta Tau Delta, 1903.

Georgia School of Technology, Atlanta, Ga.—Alpha Tau Omega, 1888; Sigma Alpha Epsilon, 1890; Kappa Sigma, 1895; Sigma Nu, 1896; Kappa Alpha, 1899; Phi Delta Theta, 1902; Chi Phi, 1904; Phi Kappa Sigma, 1904; Pi Kappa Alpha, 1904.

Georgia, University of, Athens, Ga.—Sigma Alpha Epsilon, 1866; Chi Phi, 1867; Kappa Alpha, 1868; Phi Delta Theta, 1871; Phi Gamma Delta, 1871-91; Sigma Chi, 1872-75; Sigma Nu, 1873; Alpha Tau Omega, 1878; Delta Tau Delta, 1882-99; Chi Psi, 1890; Kappa Sigma, 1901.

Grant University, Chattanooga, Tenn.—Kappa Sigma, 1882-98.

Hampden-Sidney College, Hampden-Sidney, Va.—Beta Theta Pi, 1850; Phi Kappa Psi, 1855-00; Sigma Alpha Epsilon, 1860-61;

Chi Phi, 1867; Phi Gamma Delta, 1870-04; Sigma Chi, 1872-02: Kappa Sigma, 1883; Pi Kappa Alpha, 1885; Alpha Tau Omega, 1890-96; Kappa Alpha, 1899.

Harvard University, Cambridge, Mass.—Alpha Delta Phi, 1837; Beta Theta Pi, 1843-01; Delta Phi, 1845-01; Psi Upsilon, 1850-72; Delta Kappa Epsilon, 1851-91; Zeta Psi, 1852-92; Theta Delta Chi, 1856; Phi Kappa Sigma, 1865-65; Delta Upsilon, 1880; Chi Phi, 1885-87; Sigma Alpha Epsilon, 1893, Kappa Sigma, 1905.

Idaho, University of, Moscow, Idaho.—Kappa Sigma, 1905.

Illinois, University of, Urbana, Ill.—Delta Tau Delta, 1872; Sigma Chi, 1881; Kappa Sigma, 1891; Phi Kappa Sigma, 1892; Phi Delta Theta, 1893; Alpha Tau Omega, 1895; Phi Gamma Delta, 1897; Sigma Alpha Epsilon, 1899; Beta Theta Pi, 1902; Sigma Nu, 1902; Sigma Phi Epsilon, 1903; Phi Kappa Psi, 1904; Delta Kappa Epsilon, 1904; Delta Upsilon, 1905.

Indiana University, Bloomington, Ind.—Beta Theta Pi, 1845; Phi Delta Theta, 1849; Sigma Chi, 1858; Phi Kappa Psi, 1869; Delta Tau Delta, 1870; Phi Gamma Delta, 1871; Kappa Sigma, 1887; Sigma Nu, 1892.

Indianapolis, University of, Indianapolis, Ind., and Irvington, Ind.—Phi Delta Theta, 1859; Sigma Chi, 1865; Delta Tau Delta, 1875; Beta Theta Pi, 1878-81; Kappa Sigma, 1891-93.

Iowa, University of, Iowa City, Ia.—Beta Theta Pi, 1866; Phi Kappa Psi, 1867-85; Phi Gamma Delta, 1873-73; Delta Tau Delta, 1880; Phi Delta Theta, 1882; Sigma Chi, 1882; Sigma Nu, 1893; Alpha Chi Rho, 1899-02; Kappa Sigma, 1902; Sigma Alpha Epsilon, 1904.

Kentucky State College, Lexington, Ky.—Kappa Alpha, 1893; Sigma Chi, 1893; Sigma Alpha Epsilon, 1900; Pi Kappa Alpha, 1901; Kappa Sigma, 1901; Phi Delta Theta, 1901; Sigma Nu. 1902.

Kentucky University, Lexington, Ky.—Phi Gamma Delta, 1860-62; Phi Kappa Psi, 1865-66; Pi Kappa Alpha, 1887; Kappa Alpha, 1891; Kappa Sigma, 1894-1901.

Lake Forest University, Lake Forest, Ill.—Kappa Sigma, 1880.

Lehigh University, Bethlehem, Pa.—Phi Kappa Sigma, 1870-87; Chi Phi, 1872; Delta Tau Delta, 1874; Phi Delta Theta, 1876;

Alpha Tau Omega, 1882; Delta Phi, 1884; Psi Upsilon, 1884; Theta Delta Chi, 1884; Delta Upsilon, 1885; Sigma Nu, 1885; Sigma Phi, 1886; Phi Gamma Delta, 1887; Sigma Chi, 1887; Beta Theta Pi, 1890; Chi Phi, 1893; Kappa Alpha, 1894; Kappa Sigma, 1900; Phi Sigma Kappa, 1901.

Louisiana State University, Baton Rouge, La.—Sigma Alpha Epsilon, 1867; Kappa Alpha, 1885; Kappa Sigma, 1887; Sigma Nu, 1887; Pi Kappa Alpha, 1903.

Maine, University of, Orono, Me.—Beta Theta Pi, 1878; Kappa Sigma, 1885; Alpha Tau Omega, 1891; Phi Kappa Sigma, 1898; Phi Gamma Delta, 1899; Sigma Alpha Epsilon, 1901; Sigma Chi, 1902.

Maryland Military and Naval Academy, Oxford, Md.—Kappa Sigma, 1885-87.

Maryland, University of, Baltimore, Md.—Kappa Sigma, 1873; Phi Gamma Delta, 1879-83; Phi Sigma Kappa, 1897; Phi Kappa Sigma, 1899.

Massachusetts State College, Amherst, Mass.—Q. T. V., 1869; Phi Sigma Kappa, 1873; Kappa Sigma, 1904.

Mercer University, Macon, Ga.—Chi Phi, 1869-80; Sigma Alpha Epsilon, 1870; Phi Delta Theta, 1872; Kappa Alpha, 1873; Kappa Sigma, 1875; Alpha Tau Omega, 1880; Sigma Nu, 1884.

Michigan, University of, Ann Arbor, Mich.—Beta Theta Pi, 1845; Chi Psi, 1845; Alpha Delta Phi, 1846; Delta Kappa Epsilon, 1855; Delta Phi, 1855-77; Zeta Psi, 1858; Sigma Phi, 1858; Phi Delta Theta, 1864; Psi Upsilon, 1865; Delta Tau Delta, 1871; Phi Kappa Psi, 1876; Delta Upsilon, 1876; Sigma Chi, 1877; Chi Phi, 1882-85; Phi Gamma Delta, 1885; Alpha Tau Omega, 1888-94; Sigma Alpha Epsilon, 1889; Theta Delta Chi, 1889; Kappa Sigma, 1892; Sigma Nu, 1902.

Millsaps College, Jackson, Miss.—Kappa Alpha, 1893; Kappa Sigma, 1895; Pi Kappa Alpha, 1905.

Minnesota, University of, Minneapolis, Minn.—Chi Psi, 1874; Phi Delta Theta, 1881; Delta Tau Delta, 1883; Sigma Chi, 1888; Phi Kappa Psi, 1888; Phi Gamma Delta, 1889; Beta Theta Pi, 1890; Delta Upsilon, 1890; Psi Upsilon, 1891; Theta Delta Chi, 1892; Alpha Delta Phi, 1892; Zeta Psi, 1899; Kappa Sigma, 1901;

Alpha Tau Omega, 1902; Sigma Alpha Epsilon, 1902; Sigma Nu, 1904.

Missouri School of Mines, Rolla, Mo.—Kappa Alpha, 1903; Sigma Nu, 1903; Kappa Sigma, 1903; Pi Kappa Alpha, 1906.

Missouri, University of, Columbia, Mo.—Phi Kappa Psi, 1869-74; Phi Delta Theta, 1870; Sigma Alpha Epsilon, 1884; Sigma Nu, 1886; Beta Theta Pi, 1890; Kappa Alpha, 1891; Sigma Chi, 1896; Kappa Sigma, 1898; Phi Gamma Delta, 1899; Delta Tau Delta, 1905; Alpha Tau Omega, 1906.

Nebraska, University of, Lincoln, Neb.—Phi Delta Theta, 1875; Sigma Chi, 1883; Beta Theta Pi, 1888; Sigma Alpha Epsilon, 1893; Delta Tau Delta, 1894; Phi Kappa Psi, 1895; Alpha Tau Omega, 1897; Kappa Sigma, 1897; Delta Upsilon, 1898; Phi Gamma Delta, 1898.

New Hampshire College, Durham, N. H.—Kappa Sigma, 1901.

New York University, New York, N. Y.—Sigma Phi, 1835-48; Alpha Delta Phi, 1835-39; Psi Upsilon, 1837; Delta Phi, 1841; Zeta Psi, 1847; Delta Psi, 1847-53; Delta Upsilon, 1865; Phi Gamma Delta, 1892; Kappa Sigma, 1905.

North Carolina A. and M. College, Raleigh, N. C.—Sigma Nu, 1895; Kappa Sigma, 1903; Kappa Alpha, 1903; Pi Kappa Alpha, 1904; Sigma Phi Epsilon, 1905.

North Carolina, University of, Chapel Hill, N. C.—Delta Kappa Epsilon, 1851; Phi Gamma Delta, 1851-98; Beta Theta Pi, 1851; Delta Psi, 1854-62; Delta Phi, 1855-61; Chi Psi, 1855-61; Phi Kappa Sigma, 1856-95; Sigma Alpha Epsilon, 1857; Theta Delta Chi, 1857-62; Zeta Psi, 1858; Chi Phi, 1858-68; Alpha Tau Omega, 1879; Kappa Alpha, 1881; Phi Delta Theta, 1885; Sigma Nu, 1888; Sigma Chi, 1889-00; Kappa Sigma. 1893; Pi Kappa Alpha, 1895; Sigma Phi Epsilon, 1906.

North Georgia Agricultural College, Dahlonega, Ga.—Sigma Alpha Epsilon, 1879-88; Sigma Nu, 1881; Kappa Sigma, 1885-91; Pi Kappa Alpha, 1900.

Ohio Northern University, Ada, Ohio.—Kappa Sigma, 1886-88; Sigma Phi Epsilon, 1905.

Ohio State University, Columbus, Ohio.—Phi Gamma Delta. 1878; Phi Kappa Psi, 1880; Sigma Chi, 1882; Chi Phi, 1883; Phi Delta Theta, 1883; Beta Theta Pi, 1885; Sigma Nu, 1891;

Alpha Tau Omega, 1892; Sigma Alpha Epsilon, 1892; Delta Tau Delta, 1894; Kappa Sigma, 1895; Delta Upsilon, 1904.

Oklahoma, University of, Norman, Okla.—Kappa Alpha, 1906; Kappa Sigma, 1906.

Oregon, University of, Eugene, Ore.—Sigma Nu, 1900; Kappa Sigma, 1904.

Pennsylvania State College, State College, Pa.—Delta Tau Delta, 1872-73; Beta Theta Pi, 1888; Phi Gamma Delta, 1888; Phi Kappa Sigma, 1890; Sigma Chi, 1891; Kappa Sigma, 1892; Sigma Alpha Epsilon, 1892; Phi Sigma Kappa, 1899; Phi Delta Theta, 1904.

Pennsylvania, University of, Philadelphia, Pa.—Delta Phi, 1849; Zeta Psi, 1850; Phi Kappa Sigma, 1850; Delta Psi, 1854; Sigma Chi, 1875; Phi Kappa Psi, 1877; Beta Theta Pi, 1880; Alpha Tau Omega, 1881; Phi Gamma Delta, 1881; Chi Phi, 1883-85; Phi Delta Theta, 1883; Delta Upsilon, 1888; Psi Upsilon, 1891; Kappa Sigma, 1892; Sigma Nu, 1894; Alpha Chi Rho, 1896; Delta Tau Delta, 1897; Delta Kappa Epsilon, 1898; Phi Sigma Kappa, 1900; Sigma Alpha Epsilon, 1901; Sigma Phi Epsilon, 1904.

Purdue University, Lafayette, Ind.—Sigma Chi, 1875; Kappa Sigma, 1885; Phi Delta Theta, 1893; Sigma Nu, 1891; Sigma Alpha Epsilon, 1893; Phi Kappa Psi, 1901; Phi Gamma Delta, 1902; Beta Theta Pi, 1903; Alpha Tau Omega, 1904; Phi Kappa Sigma, 1905.

Randolph-Macon College, Ashland, Va.—Delta Psi, 1853-61; Kappa Alpha, 1869; Phi Kappa Psi, 1870-82; Phi Kappa Sigma, 1872; Beta Theta Pi, 1873-93; Sigma Chi, 1874-01; Phi Delta Theta, 1874; Kappa Sigma, 1888.

Richmond College, Richmond, Va.—Beta Theta Pi, 1870-96; Kappa Alpha, 1870; Phi Kappa Sigma, 1873; Phi Delta Theta, 1875-95; Alpha Tau Omega, 1878-82; Sigma Chi, 1880-81; Sigma Alpha Epsilon, 1884-87; Phi Gamma Delta, 1890; Pi Kappa Alpha, 1891; Kappa Sigma, 1898; Sigma Phi Epsilon, 1901.

South Carolina College, Columbia, S. C.—Delta Psi, 1850-61; Delta Kappa Epsilon, 1852-61; Phi Kappa Psi, 1857-93; Chi Psi, 1858-97; Beta Theta Pi, 1858-61; Theta Delta Chi, 1859-61; Kappa Alpha, 1880-97; Sigma Alpha Epsilon, 1882-97; Phi

Delta Theta, 1882-93; Alpha Tau Omega, 1883-97; Sigma Nu, 1886-97; Chi Phi, 1889-97; Kappa Sigma, 1890-97; Pi Kappa Alpha, 1891-97.

Southwestern Baptist University (West Tennessee College, Jackson, Tenn., and *Union University,* Murfreesboro, Tenn., were united to form *Southwestern Baptist University),* Jackson, Tenn.—At *Union University,* Phi Gamma Delta, 1851-73; Sigma Alpha Epsilon, 1857-72; Delta Kappa Epsilon, 1860-62; Alpha Tau Omega, 1867-73. At *West Tennessee College,* Sigma Alpha Epsilon, 1867-70. At *Southwestern Baptist University,* Sigma Alpha Epsilon, 1878; Kappa Sigma, 1892; Alpha Tau Omega, 1894.

Southwestern Presbyterian University, Clarksville, Tenn.—Pi Kappa Alpha, 1878; Kappa Sigma, 1882; Alpha Tau Omega, 1882; Sigma Alpha Epsilon, 1882; Kappa Alpha, 1887-1905.

Southwestern University, Georgetown, Tex.—Kappa Alpha, 1883; Kappa Sigma, 1886; Phi Delta Theta, 1886; Sigma Alpha Epsilon, 1887-88.

Stanford University, Stanford University, Cal.—Zeta Psi, 1891; Phi Delta Theta, 1891; Phi Kappa Psi, 1891; Sigma Nu, 1891; Sigma Chi, 1891; Alpha Tau Omega, 1891-97; Sigma Alpha Epsilon, 1892; Delta Tau Delta, 1893; Beta Theta Pi, 1894; Chi Psi, 1895; Kappa Alpha, 1895; Delta Upsilon, 1896; Kappa Sigma, 1899; Delta Kappa Epsilon, 1901; Theta Delta Chi, 1903; Phi Gamma Delta, 1903.

Swarthmore College, Swarthmore, Pa.—Kappa Sigma, 1888; Phi Kappa Psi, 1889; Delta Upsilon, 1893; Phi Sigma Kappa, 1906.

Syracuse, University of, Syracuse, N. Y.—Delta Kappa Epsilon, 1871; Delta Upsilon, 1873; Zeta Psi, 1875; Psi Upsilon, 1875; Phi Kappa Psi, 1883; Phi Delta Theta, 1887; Beta Theta Pi, 1889; Phi Gamma Delta, 1901; Sigma Chi, 1904; Sigma Nu, 1905; Sigma Phi Epsilon, 1906; Kappa Sigma, 1906.

Tennessee, University of, Knoxville, Tenn.—Alpha Tau Omega, 1872; Pi Kappa Alpha, 1874; Sigma Alpha Epsilon, 1879; Kappa Sigma, 1880; Kappa Alpha, 1883; Phi Gamma Delta, 1890.

Texas, University of, Austin, Tex.—Kappa Alpha, 1883; Phi

Delta Theta, 1883; Phi Gamma Delta, 1883; Kappa Sigma, 1884; Sigma Alpha Epsilon, 1884; Sigma Chi, 1885; Beta Theta Pi, 1886; Sigma Nu, 1886; Chi Phi, 1892; Alpha Tau Omega, 1897; Delta Tau Delta, 1904; Phi Kappa Psi, 1904.

Thatcher Institute, Shreveport, La.—Sigma Alpha Epsilon, 1886-88; Kappa Sigma, 1888-91.

Trinity College, Durham, N. C.—Chi Phi, 1871-79; Alpha Tau Omega, 1872; Kappa Sigma, 1873; Phi Delta Theta, 1878-79; Phi Gamma Delta, 1893; Kappa Alpha, 1901; Pi Kappa Alpha, 1901.

Tulane University of Louisiana, New Orleans, La.—Phi Kappa Sigma, 1858-61; Pi Kappa Alpha, 1878; Kappa Alpha, 1882; Sigma Chi, 1882-84; Alpha Tau Omega, 1887; Sigma Nu, 1888; Kappa Sigma, 1889; Delta Tau Delta, 1889; Phi Delta Theta, 1889; Sigma Alpha Epsilon, 1897; Delta Kappa Epsilon, 1899.

University of the South, Sewanee, Tenn.—Alpha Tau Omega, 1877; Sigma Alpha Epsilon, 1881; Kappa Sigma, 1882; Phi Delta Theta, 1883; Delta Tau Delta, 1883; Kappa Alpha, 1883; Sigma Nu, 1889-93; Pi Kappa Alpha, 1898.

Vanderbilt University, Nashville, Tenn.—Phi Delta Theta, 1876; Kappa Sigma, 1877; Sigma Alpha Epsilon, 1878; Kappa Alpha, 1883; Chi Phi, 1883-99; Beta Theta Pi, 1884; Delta Tau Delta, 1886; Sigma Nu, 1886; Alpha Tau Omega, 1889; Delta Kappa Epsilon, 1890; Sigma Chi, 1891; Pi Kappa Alpha, 1894; Phi Kappa Psi, 1901; Phi Kappa Sigma, 1902.

Vermont, University of, Burlington, Vt.—Sigma Phi, 1845; Delta Psi, 1850; Theta Delta Chi, 1852-57; Phi Delta Theta, 1879; Alpha Tau Omega, 1887; Kappa Sigma, 1893.

Virginia Polytechnic Institute, Blacksburg, Va.—Pi Kappa Alpha, 1873-80; Kappa Sigma, 1874-89; Beta Theta Pi, 1879-80.

Virginia Military Institute, Lexington, Va.—Alpha Tau Omega, 1865-81; Kappa Alpha, 1868-88; Beta Theta Pi, 1869-80; Sigma Nu, 1869-88; Kappa Sigma, 1874-83; Sigma Alpha Epsilon, 1874; Phi Delta Theta, 1878-89; Sigma Chi, 1884-85.

Virginia, University of, Charlottesville, Va.—Delta Kappa Epsilon, 1852; Phi Kappa Psi, 1853; Phi Kappa Sigma, 1855; Beta Theta Pi, 1856; Kappa Alpha, (N. O.), 1857-61; Sigma Alpha Epsilon, 1857; Phi Gamma Delta, 1859; Chi Phi, 1859; Chi Psi,

1860-70; Sigma Chi, 1860; Delta Psi, 1860; Zeta Psi, 1868; Pi Kappa Alpha, 1868; Alpha Tau Omega, 1868; Kappa Sigma, 1869; Sigma Nu, 1870; Theta Delta Chi, 1875-77; Kappa Alpha (S. O.), 1873; Phi Delta Theta, 1873; Delta Tau Delta, 1888.

Wabash College, Crawfordsville, Ind.—Beta Theta Pi, 1846; Phi Delta Theta, 1850; Phi Gamma Delta, 1866; Phi Kappa Psi, 1870-00; Delta Tau Delta, 1872; Theta Delta Chi, 1879-82; Sigma Chi, 1880-94; Kappa Sigma, 1895.

Washington and Jefferson College, Washington, Pa.—Beta Theta Pi, 1842; Phi Gamma Delta, 1848; Phi Kappa Psi, 1852; Phi Kappa Sigma, 1854; Sigma Chi, 1858-69; Delta Kappa Epsilon, 1858-65; Delta Upsilon, 1858-70; Theta Delta Chi, 1858-72; Delta Tau Delta, 1861; Phi Delta Theta, 1875; Alpha Tau Omega, 1882; Kappa Sigma, 1898; Sigma Phi Epsilon, 1898-06.

Washington and Lee University, Lexington, Va.—Phi Kappa Psi, 1855; Beta Theta Pi, 1856-80; Alpha Tau Omega, 1865; Kappa Alpha, 1865; Sigma Chi, 1866; Sigma Alpha Epsilon, 1867; Delta Kappa Epsilon, 1867-78; Phi Gamma Delta, 1868; Delta Psi, 1869-88; Theta Delta Chi, 1869-74; Delta Psi, 1869-88; Theta Delta Chi, 1869-74; Chi Phi, 1872-75; Kappa Sigma, 1873; Sigma Nu, 1882; Phi Delta Theta, 1887; Pi Kappa Alpha, 1892; Phi Kappa Sigma, 1893; Delta Tau Delta, 1896; Sigma Phi Epsilon, 1906.

Washington University, St. Louis, Mo.—Beta Theta Pi, 1869; Phi Delta Theta, 1891; Sigma Alpha Epsilon, 1892; Kappa Sigma, 1902; Sigma Chi, 1903; Sigma Nu, 1903; Kappa Alpha, 1906.

Washington, University of, Seattle, Wash.—Sigma Nu, 1896; Phi Gamma Delta, 1900; Phi Delta Theta, 1900; Beta Theta Pi, 1901; Sigma Chi, 1903; Kappa Sigma, 1903; Sigma Alpha Epsilon, 1906; Alpha Tau Omega, 1906.

West Virginia, University of, Morgantown, W. Va.—Kappa Sigma, 1883-87; Phi Kappa Psi, 1890; Phi Sigma Kappa, 1891; Sigma Chi, 1895; Phi Kappa Sigma, 1896; Kappa Alpha, 1897; Beta Theta Pi, 1900; Delta Tau Delta, 1901; Sigma Phi Epsilon, 1903; Sigma Nu, 1904; Pi Kappa Alpha, 1904.

William Jewell College, Liberty, Mo.—Phi Gamma Delta, 1886; Kappa Alpha, 1887; Sigma Nu, 1894; Kappa Sigma, 1897.

William and Mary College, Williamsburg, Va.—Theta Delta Chi, 1853; Sigma Alpha Epsilon, 1858-61; Pi Kappa Alpha, 1871; Beta Theta Pi, 1874-77; Kappa Alpha, 1890; Kappa Sigma, 1890; Sigma Phi Epsilon, 1904.

Wisconsin, University of, Madison, Wis.—Phi Delta Theta, 1857; Beta Theta Pi, 1873; Phi Kappa Psi, 1875; Chi Psi, 1878; Delta Upsilon, 1883; Sigma Chi, 1884; Delta Tau Delta, 1888; Phi Gamma Delta, 1893; Theta Delta Chi, 1895; Psi Upsilon, 1896; Kappa Sigma, 1898; Phi Kappa Sigma, 1901; Sigma Nu, 1902; Alpha Delta Phi, 1903; Sigma Alpha Epsilon, 1903.

Wofford College, Spartanburg, S. C.—Kappa Alpha, 1869; Chi Psi, 1869; Chi Phi, 1871; Phi Delta Theta, 1879-84; Sigma Alpha Epsilon, 1885; Pi Kappa Alpha, 1891; Alpha Tau Omega, 1891-94; Kappa Sigma, 1894.

APPENDIX B

THE CHAPTERS

In the sources of the Fraternity's history—magazine articles, Conclave reports, and Catalogues—there are various sketches of how Chapters came into existence, and their subsequent history. The following gives some condensed information upon each Chapter—its founders, charter members, dates of existence, number of initiates and deceased members:

ZETA, parent chapter. Established at the University of Virginia, Charlottesville, Va., on December 10, 1869. Founders: William Grigsby McCormick, George Miles Arnold, Edmund Law Rogers, Frank Courtney Nicodemus, and John Covert Boyd. Total number of initiates, 165; deceased members, 22.

BETA, second chapter chartered. Established at the University of Alabama, Tuscaloosa, Ala., in 1871. Probably became inactive in 1871 by anti-fraternity legislation; was reestablished on June 3, 1899. Sponsor at establishment: George Wyatt Hollingsworth. Charter members: George Wyatt Hollingsworth and others. Records lost or destroyed. Sponsor at reestablishment in 1899: Nathaniel Leslie Carpenter (Vanderbilt). Total number of initiates, 68, deceased members, 2.

ETA PRIME, third chapter chartered. Established at Trinity College, N. C., on February 28, 1873. Became inactive in 1879 by anti-fraternity legislation; was reestablished on December 1, 1892. Sponsor at establishment: James H. Durham (Virginia). Charter members: Thomas Taylor, Adolphus Richard Wortham, Ned. H. Tucker, Peter Edmond Hines, George David Tysor and William Parker Mercer. Sponsors at reestablishment in 1892: Herbert Milton Martin (Randolph-Macon), Williamson Wallace Morris (Davidson), and James Davidson McDowell (Davidson). Total number of initiates, 118; deceased members, 14.

MU, fourth chapter chartered. Established at Washington and Lee University, Lexington, Va., in December, 1873. Became inactive in 1876, was reestablished on September 10, 1888. Charter withdrawn in 1900; was again reestablished on March 11, 1904, absorbing the local chapter of Mu Pi Lambda. Sponsor at establishment: Euclid Lane Johnson (Virginia). Charter members: John Nathaniel Prather, William Templeton Durrett, Griffin Johnston, and Henry Conyers Payne. Sponsor at reestablishment in 1888: James Taylor McCaa. Sponsors at reestablishment in 1904: Herbert Milton Martin (Randolph-Macon), Stanley Watkins Martin (Virginia Polytechnic), James David Johnston (Emory and Henry), Robert Leigh Owen (Hampden-Sidney), Richard Cralle Stokes (Hampden-Sidney), George Washington Headley, Jr., (Kentucky State), Harry Wall (Virginia), James Archer Sellman (Virginia), Frederick Gresham Pollard (Richmond), Sanford Burnell Bragg (Richmond), Olin Lecato McMath (Randolph-Macon College), and Thomas Peachy Spencer (William and Mary). Total number of initiates, 90; deceased members, 6.

XI, fifth chapter chartered. Established at the Virginia Military Institute, Lexington, Va., on January 3, 1874. Became inactive in 1884 through anti-fraternity laws, since which time it has not been re-established. Anti-fraternity laws obtain. Sponsors at establishment: John Nathaniel Prather, William Templeton Durrett, Griffin Johnston and Henry Conyers Payne, all of Washington and Lee. Charter members: Jefferson Davis, Jr., Henry Taylor Earnest, John Ashley Taylor, Sterling Woodward Tucker, Robert Henry Watkins, J. L. Butler, and Frazor Titus Edmondson. Total number of initiates, 23; deceased members, 9.

NU, sixth chapter chartered. Established at the Virginia Polytechnic Institute, Blacksburg, Va., on June 17, 1874. Became inactive in 1889 by reason of anti-fraternity laws. Anti-fraternity laws obtain. Sponsor at establishment: Stephen Alonzo Jackson (Virginia). Charter members: Adoniram Judson Evans, Robert Peyton Bayley, William Freneau Page, William Augustus Edwards, Charles Edward Wingo, Harry Marston Smith, Jr., John William Cowherd, Walter Gardner Lane, William Bachelor Farant, and John Marshall Warwick. Total number of initiates, 91; deceased members, 12.

OMICRON, seventh chapter chartered. Established at Emory and Henry College, Emory, Va., on June 24, 1874. Became inactive in 1895 by reason of anti-fraternity laws. Anti-fraternity laws obtain. Sponsor at establishment: Stephen Alonzo Jackson (Virginia). Charter members: Abel Chapman, Samuel P. Neal, Robert Edmondson Buchanan, Samuel Beattie Ryburn Dunn, Barton Stone, Benjamin Patterson Sanders, Russell C. Rose, and Edmund Tracy Nicholas. Total number of initiates, 138; deceased members, 24.

ALPHA-ALPHA, eighth chapter chartered. Established at the University of Maryland, Baltimore, Md., on November 28, 1874. Charter withdrawn in 1875; was reestablished on December 31, 1890; became inactive in 1892; and was again reestablished on February 25, 1898. Sponsor at establishment: Arthur Cowton Heffenger (Virginia). Charter members: Arthur Cowton Heffenger, William Baldwin Beach, Aaron Fenton, Washington Clement Claude, Joseph Bucey Galloway, Henry Davidson Fry, William Greensbury Goldsborough Wilson, Stephen Olin Richey, and Thomas Kelly Galloway. Sponsors at reestablishment in 1890: C. B. Burke (Md. Mil. and Nav.), and delegates to the Ninth Biennial G. Convlave. Sponsors at reestablishment in 1898: Hamilton Janney Coffroth clave. Sponsors at reestablishment in 1898: Hamilton Janney Coffroth (Virginia Military Institute), Eldridge Eakin Wolff (Randolph-Macon), Oscar Leslie Rogers (Mercer), Edwin Curtis Hamilton (Emory and Henry), and Edward Roland Hart (North Carolina). Total number of initiates, 100; deceased members, 5.

ALPHA-BETA, ninth chapter chartered. Established at Mercer University, Macon, Ga., in 1875. Became inactive in 1879; was reestablished on September 28, 1891. Sponsor at establishment: William Anderson Thomas (Trinity). Charter members: William Anderson Thomas, Charles Hyatt Richardson, Charles Henry Spurgeon Jackson, Chovine Clegg Richardson, and Seaborn W. Wright. Sponsors at reestablishment in 1891: Stephen Alonzo Jackson (Virginia), Robert Ernest Dart (North Georgia), James Wesley Crump (Sewanee), Iverson Louis Harris (Mercer), and Francis William Hazlehurst (Maryland Military and Naval). Total number of initiates, 93; deceased members, 1.

KAPPA, tenth chapter chartered. Established at Vanderbilt University, Nashville, Tenn., on April 13, 1877. Became inactive in 1880 by reason of anti-fraternity laws; was re-established on January 20, 1885. Sponsors at establishment: James Quinn Moore (Emory and Henry), David Rankin Stubblefield (Emory and Henry) and Mora Hammond Sharpe (Emory and Henry). Charter members: James Quinn Moore, David Rankin Stubblefield, Mora Hammond Sharpe, James Hill Scaife, and Joseph Franklin Dowdy. Sponsors at reestablishment in 1885: Frank Goodman (Tennessee), Walter Scott Ayres (Emory and Henry), Henry Bruce Buckner (Sewanee), Charles Wiles Thompson (Sewanee), William Cozart Phillips (Sewanee), Jesse Farrell Sugg (Tennessee), Thomas Rice Allen (Tennessee), James Milton Patterson (Tennessee), and Hugh Mott Dunlop (Southwestern Presbyterian). Total number of initiates, 160; deceased members, 15.

LAMBDA, eleventh chapter chartered. Established at the University of Tennessee, Knoxville, Tenn., on May 11, 1880. Sponsors at establishment: Stephen Alonzo Jackson (Virginia), and James Paris McMillan (Emory and Henry). Charter members: James Paris McMillan, Richard McKenney, Charles Floyd Humes and Thomas Shields Vaden. Total number of initiates, 192; deceased members, 24.

ALPHA-CHI, twelfth chapter chartered. Established at Lake Forest University, Lake Forest, Ill., on Oct. 23, 1880. Became inactive in 1882 by reason of anti-fraternity laws; was reestablished on Nov. 25, 1896. Local society Lambda Phi absorbed in 1896. Sponsor at establishment: Alexander Chalmers McNeil (Emory and Henry). Charter members: Alexander Chalmers McNeil, Charles Alexander Evans, John Dudley Pope, Frederick Robinson, Jr., and George Thomson. Sponsors at reestablishment in 1896: Alfred Bolander Loranz (Wabash), Hugh Miller (Wabash), Charles Brewster Randolph (Cumberland), and Robert Elberon Dunlop (Wabash). Total number of initiates, 68; deceased members, 2.

ALPHA-IOTA, thirteenth chapter chartered. Established at Grant University, Athens, Tenn., on Feb. 15, 1882. Charter withdrawn in 1883; was reestablished on May 13, 1892 by absorption of the local society the "Secret Fraternity;" and again became inactive in 1898 by the withdrawal of its charter. Anti-fraternity laws do not obtain. Sponsor at establishment: Stephen Alonzo Jackson (Virginia). Charter Members: Samuel Washington McCallie, and Samuel Bruce La Rue. Sponsors at reestablishment in 1892: John Jay Bernard (Tennessee), Robert Wood Tate (Tennessee), William Andrew McCord (Tennessee), Thomas Jefferson Brown (Tennessee), and Alfred Young Bailey (Tennessee). Total number of initiates, 43; deceased members, 2.

PHI, fourteenth chapter chartered. Established at Southwestern Presbyterian University, Clarksville, Tenn., on April 12, 1882. Sponsor at establishment: Stephen Alonzo Jackson (Virginia). Charter members: Carrington Mason, Jr., Henry Craft, Jr., and Dudley Thomas Schoolfield. Total number of initiates, 116; deceased members, 4.

OMEGA, fifteenth chapter chartered. Established at the University of the South, Sewanee, Tenn., on May 6, 1882. Sponsors at establishment: Stephen Alonzo Jackson (Virginia) and Arthur Mason Chichester (Virginia). Charter members: Arthur Mason Chichester, William Henry Inglesby, George Davis Footman, George Anderson Waddill, Alfred Menard Moulton, Inman Horner Knox, Morris Kerr Clark, Lee Brock, Edward Walter Hughes, Edward Elliott Camber Habersham, Frederick D. Halsey, Charles Chaffe, and Elard Ferdinand von Ende. Total number of initiates, 175; deceased members, 21.

PI, sixteenth chapter chartered. Established at the University of West Virginia, Morgantown, W. Va., in Sept., 1883. Became inactive in 1887, since which time it has not been revived. Anti-fraternity laws do not obtain. Sponsor at establishment: Stephen Alonzo Jackson (Virginia). Charter members: John Goodloe Jackson, Robert E. Jackson, Winston Henry Hoffman, William Jacob Johnson, and Blackwell Chilton Wilson. Total number of initiates, 17; deceased members, 1.

UPSILON, seventeenth chapter chartered. Established at Hampden-Sidney College, Prince Edward County, Va., on Nov. 14, 1883. Local society, Phi Mu Gamma, absorbed. Sponsor at establishment: Stephen Alonzo Jackson (Virginia). Charter members: Alexander Lee Bondurant, George Keatts Mason, John Harvie Hull, William Taylor Thayer, Jr., and John Marion Hart, Jr. Total number of initiates, 94; deceased members, 8.

TAU, eighteenth chapter chartered. Established at the University of Texas, Austin, Texas, on Sept. 18, 1884. Sponsor at establishment: Walter Lee Robertson (Sewanee). Charter members: Rhodes Fisher, Jr., Isaac Jalonick, Frederick Carlos von Rosenberg, Isaac V. Davis, and Rufus Atwood Palm. Total number of initiates, 205; deceased members, 11.

RHO, nineteenth chapter chartered. Established at the North Georgia Agricultural College, Dahlonega, Ga., on Feb. 11, 1885. Became inactive in 1891, since which time it has not been reestablished. Anti-fraternity laws do not obtain. Sponsors at establishment: William Henry Inglesby (Sewanee), Stephen Alonzo Jackson (Virginia), and John Newton Humes (Emory and Henry). Charter members: Edward Lee Sutton, Edward Cornelius Cartledge, James Beverly Martin, William Thomas Shockley, Charles Hill Rawlins, James Paul Stribling, Charles Daniel McRae, and Homer Brown Cobb. Total number of initiates, 32; deceased members, 2.

CHI, twentieth chapter chartered. Established at Purdue University, Lafayette, Ind., on March 15, 1885. Sponsors at establishment: Augustus Ruffner (West Virginia), and William Taylor Thayer, Jr. (Hampden-Sidney). Charter members: Augustus Ruffner, William Taylor Thayer, Jr., Michael Steele Bright, Oscar Ulysses Mutz, and James Sydney Boyd. Total number of initiates, 166; deceased members, 9.

DELTA, twenty-first chapter chartered. Established at the Maryland Military and Naval Academy, Oxford, Md., on Oct. 19, 1885. Charter withdrawn in 1887, because of closing of institution. Sponsor at establishment: Frederick Carlos von Rosenberg (Texas). Charter members: Frederick Carlos von Rosenberg, Francis William Hazlehurst, William Joseph Miller, Arlington Ulysses Betts, Charles Bell Burke, James Harry Covington, James Francis McIndoe, William Robert Bell, William Headly Osborne, Lawrence Low, Fletcher Bright Peters, George Lander Abell, William Martin Cooper, Charles Edward Wootten, John Harry Albright, John Wedderburn, Benjamin Rush Logie, John Henry Wagner, and Douglass Preston Rock. Total number of initiates, 31; deceased members, 2.

EPSILON, twenty-second chapter chartered. Established at Centenary College, Jackson, La., on Aug. 29, 1885. Became inactive in 1904 by tne withdrawal of its charter. Sponsors at establishment: Frank Hanson Terry (Virginia Polytechnic), and Taylor Gleaves (Virginia Polytechnic). Charter members: John Hamilton Ellis, Charles Howard Hardenbergh, Emmett Lee Irwin, Milton Sanford Standifer, and Benjamin Nathaniel Smith. Total number of initiates, 84; deceased members, 5.

PSI, twenty-third chapter chartered. Established at the University of Maine, Orono, Me., on Dec. 31, 1885. Local society, K. K. F., absorbed. Sponsor at establishment: Stephen Alonzo Jackson (Virginia). Charter members: John Decker Blagden, Henry Allan McNally, Alfred Smith Ruth, Seymour Everett Rogers, Frank Percy Collins, Josiah Murch Ayer, Gilbert Scovil Vickery, Norman Tripp, Charles Ayers Mason, Charles Benjamin Gould, and Seymore Farrington Miller. Total number of initiates, 180; deceased members, 12.

SIGMA, twenty-fourth chapter chartered. Established at the Ohio Northern University, Ada, Ohio, on May 8, 1886. Became inactive in 1888 by reason of anti-fraternity laws, since which time it has not been reestab-lished. Anti-fraternity laws do not obtain. Sponsor at establishment: Augustus Ruffner (West Virginia). Charter members: Joseph Calvin Boyd, John Elmer Virden, Elmer Ellsworth Helms, Gilbert Allison Adams, George Albert Spence, James Grant Ames, Leonidas Alvah Smith, David Channing Meck, Lawrence Hoover Seager, Bernard Daly, Frank Ells-worth Seager, Samuel Allen Hoskins, William Edie Hoover, Claudius Postean Aubert, and John Montgomery. Total number of initiates, 23; deceased members, 1.

Iota, twenty-fifth chapter chartered. Established at Southwestern University, Georgetown, Tex., on Sept. 10, 1886. Sponsor at establish-ment; Alexander Lee Bondurant (Hampden-Sydney). Charter members: Iverson Benjamin Lane, Jesse Cross Baker, Jasper Benjamin Gibbs and John Stanley Moss. Total number of initiates, 145; deceased members, 7.

Gamma, twenty-sixth chapter chartered. Established at Louisiana State University, Baton Rouge, La., on Feb. 19, 1887. Sponsors at estab-lishment: Oscar Kearney Andrews (Centenary), Thomas Ragan (Cen-tenary), Milford Sanford Standifer (Centenary), and others of the Cen-tenary Chapter. Charter members: Abel James Price, Hunter Vincent Kirkland, Roy Otto Young, Charles Graham David, and Frank Thomas Guilbeau. Total number of initiates, 139; deceased members, 6.

Alpha, twenty-seventh chapter chartered. Established at Emory Col-lege, Oxford, Ga., on March 26, 1887. Became inactive in 1891, since which time it has not been reestablished. Anti-fraternity laws do not ob-tain. Sponsor at establishment: Edward Lee Sutton (North Georgia). Charter members: Arthur Hamilton Van Dyke, Jesse Stephens Lamar, Samuel Jackson Smith, James Henry Harwell, and David Conway Gun-nels. Total number of initiates, 24; deceased members, 5.

Beta-Theta, twenty-eighth chapter chartered. Established at Indiana University, Bloomington, Ind., on May 14, 1887. Charter withdrawn in 1887; was reestablished on Feb. 10, 1900. Sponsor at establishment: William Taylor Thayer, Jr. (Hampden-Sidney). Charter members; Aaron Ellsworth Smalley, Horatio Hoop and William Herschel Bloss. Spon-sors at reestablishment in 1900: Julius Curtis Travis (Michigan), Thomas Hendricks David (Purdue), Harry Augustus Bevis (Wabash), Reginald Gates Pape (Wabash), and Samuel Elliott Perkins, Jr. (Wabash). Total number of initiates, 71; deceased members, 2.

Theta, twenty-ninth chapter chartered. Established at Cumberland University, Lebanon, Tenn., on Oct. 7, 1887. Sponsors at establishment· Henry Bruce Buckner (Sewanee), Owen Harris Wilson (Vanderbilt), and Franceway Cossitt Stratton (Vanderbilt). Charter members: Franceway Cossitt Stratton, Rufus McClain Fields, Laban Lacy Rice, Charles Marvin Hunter, Verne Clifford Armstrong, and Elvis Willard Blackmore. Total number of initiates, 123; deceased members, 6.

BETA, thirtieth chapter chartered. Established at Thatcher Institute, Shreveport, La., on February 27, 1888. Became inactive in 1891; institution closed. Sponsors at establishment: James Charles Howerton (Sewanee), and Charles Howard Hardenbergh (Centenary). Charter members: William Gregg Dalzell, Alexis Moore Lemee, Chichester Choplin, Jr., Charles Robert Caldwell, and Arthur Franklin Stephenson. Total number of initiates, 17; deceased members, 5.

PI, thirty-first chapter chartered. Established at Swarthmore College, Swarthmore, Pa., on July 21, 1888. Sponsor at establishment: William Taylor Thayer (Hampden-Sidney). Charter members: Harry Leslie Boggs, John Atkinson Thayer, Frederick Neal Carr, and Ellis Bronson Ridgway. Total number of initiates, 91; deceased members, 1.

ETA, thirty-second chapter chartered. Established at Randolph-Macon College, Ashland, Va., on Nov. 14, 1888. Sponsor at establishment: James David Johnston, Jr. (Emory and Henry). Charter members: James David Johnston, Jr., Herbert Milton Martin, Emerson Taylor Wescott, and Charles Herbert Hall. Total number of initiates, 67; deceased members, 2.

SIGMA, thirty-third chapter chartered. Established at Tulane University, New Orleans, La., on Jan. 26, 1889. Sponsors at establishment: Eugene Augustus Harris (Southwestern), Charles Howard Hardenbergh (Centenary), James Monroe Sims (Centenary), Benjamin Nathaniel Smith (Centenary), Lawrence Wade Smith (Louisiana), Abel James Price (Louisiana), Roy Otto Young (Louisiana), and Hunter Vincent Kirkland (Louisiana). Charter members: William Cyprien Dufour, Joseph Oscar Daspit, Mark Mayo Boatner, Nimrod McGuire, and Thomas McCaleb. Total number of initiates, 106; deceased members, 13.

NU, thirty-fourth chapter chartered. Established at William and Mary College, Williamsburg, Va., on March 1, 1890. Sponsors at establishment: Herbert Milton Martin (Randolph-Macon), James David Johnston, Jr. (Emory and Henry), and Harry Graham Robinson (Randolph-Macon). Charter members: Fernando Southall Farrar, Robert Southall Bright, James Brown McCaw, Killis Campbell, Harry Thompson Dozier, and John Minor Gatewood. Total number of initiates, 117; deceased members, 5.

CHI-OMEGA, thirty-fifth chapter chartered. Established at the University of South Carolina, Columbia, S. C., on April 23, 1890. Became inactive in 1897 by reason of anti-fraternity laws. Anti-fraternity laws obtain. Sponsors at establishment: Stephen Alonzo Jackson (Virginia), Crawford Clayton Wilson (Virginia), John Pegram Anderson (Virginia Polytechnic), and Samuel Macon Smith (Virginia). Charter members: William Walter Hentz, Charles Brewer, Samuel Charlton Todd, Ralph Smith, and Benjamin Palmer McMaster. Total number of initiates, 28; deceased members, 2.

XI, thirty-sixth chapter chartered. Established at the University of Arkansas, Fayetteville, Ark., on May 29, 1890. Sponsor at establishment:

Charles Richardson (Emory and Henry). Charter members: William Allen Crawford, John Clinton Futrall, Carl Clinton Miller and William Shields Goodwin. Total number of initiates, 150; deceased members, 1.

·DELTA, thirty-seventh ·chapter chartered. Established at Davidson College, Davidson, N. C., on Nov. 17, 1890. Sponsors at establishment: Charles Brewer (South Carolina), Crawford Clayton Wilson (Virginia), and Leonidas Chalmers Glenn (South Carolina). Charter members: Benjamin Waddell· Glasgow, Albert Jackson Wittson, Williamson ·Wallace Morris, ·Charles Lester Grey, Robert Junius Hunter, and William Alexander Hafner. Total number of initiates, 97; deceased members, 0.

BETA, thirty-eighth chapter chartered. Established at Butler· .University, Irvington, Ind., on Feb. 16, 1891. Charter surrendered in 1893, since which time it has not been reestablished. Anti-fraternity laws do not obtain. Sponsors at establishment: Samuel Kennedy, Arthur Graydon Moody, Wilbur Nathaniel Morrill, Robert Allen Lackey, Charles Archibald Murray, Charles Morgan Olds, John Erhard Muhlfeld, Job Lyndon Van Natta, Willard Cheney Knight, William Howard Aldrich, Jr., Russell Spencer Viberg and James Vinton Godman, all of Purdue. Charter members: James Dennis Carson, Mark Antony Collips, Jesse Lincoln Brady, George Varner Miller, Robert Philson Collins, and Charles Manker. Total number of initiates, 11; deceased members, 0.

ALPHA-GAMMA, thirty-ninth chapter chartered. Established at the University of Illinois, Champaign, Ill., on Nov. 17, 1891. Sponsor at establishment: Robert Allen Lackey (Purdue). Charter members: James Steele, William George Miller, William Ernest Steinwedell, George Phil'p Behrensmeyer, Frank David Arms, James David Metcalf, and George Herbert Atherton. Total number of initiates, 159; deceased members, 4.

ALPHA-DELTA, fortieth chapter chartered.. Established at the Pennsylvania State College, State College, Pa., on Jan. 8, 1892. Sponsors at establishment: Frederick Neal Carr (Swarthmore), Frederic William Speakman (Swarthmore), Walter Weaver Hibbert (Swarthmore), and Robert Woodward Lippincott (Swarthmore). Charter members: Milton Speer McDowell, William Powell Rothrock, Walter Blair Waite, Mark Truman Swartz, Hugh Stuart Taylor and Arthur George Guyer. Total number of initiates, 121; deceased members, 2.

ALPHA-EPSILON, forty-first chapter chartered. Established at the University of Pennsylvania, Philadelphia, Pa., on Jan. 20, 1892. Sponsors at establishment: James Harry Covington (Maryland Military and Naval), Frank Ross Sherard (Washington and Lee), Montgomery Gano Buckner (Texas), Alfred Burwell Claytor (Washington and Lee), and members of Pi Chapter, Swarthmore College, and others. Charter members: James Harry Covington, Frank Ross Sherard, Montgomery Gano Buckner, and Alfred Burwell Claytor. Total number of initiates, 111; deceased members, 1.

APPENDIX B 149

ALPHA-ZETA, forty-second chapter chartered. Established at the University of Michigan, Ann Arbor, Mich., on Feb. 23, 1892. Sponsors at establishment: Alexander Yerger Scott (Sewanee), Daniel Edward Storms (Purdue), and George Frank Rich (Maine). Charter members: Alexander Yerger Scott, Daniel Edward Storms, George Frank Rich, Lyman Gaston Grundy,. Albert Mahlon Ashley, Jesse Elmer Roberts, Julian Alvin Padgett, Richard Francis Purcell, Anson Daniel Rose, and Horatio Vallandigham Gard. Total number of initiates. 147; deceased members, 5.

ALPHA-ETA, forty-third chapter chartered. Established at George Washington University, Washington, D. C., on Feb. 23, 1892. Became inactive in 1893; was reestablished on May 28, 1896. Sponsors at establishment: Schiller Brents Hermann (Washington and Lee), Albert Jackson Wittson (Davidson), William Homer Greer (Washington and Lee), Angus McDonald (Virginia), John Benjamin Clark (North Georgia), William Cowan Bowen (Maryland), William Bolivar Byers (Maryland), Albert C. Stephens (Maryland), and John Halsey Phillips (North Georgia). Charter members: Edward Grant Seibert, -Clarence George Probert, Lincoln Johnson, and Van Buren Knott: Sponsors at reestablishment: Robert Henry Tucker (William and Mary), John Womack Wright (William and Mary), John Howard Allen (Vanderbilt), William Thompson Pollard (Randolph-Macon), and George Coleman Bushnell (Cumberland). Total number of initiates, 132; deceased members, 7.

ALPHA-THETA, forty-fourth chapter chartered. Established at Southwestern Baptist University, Jackson, Tenn., on March 5, 1892. Sponsors at establishment: Charles Bell Burke (Maryland Military and Naval), John Cullom Wilson (Vanderbilt), George Harris Robertson (Southwestern Presbyterian), John Chester Botts (Southwestern Presbyterian), and Martin Holbrook (Tennessee). Charter members: John Collum Wilson, John Whittaker Buford, Jr., Jere Lawrence Crook, Flarnc Lee Dennison, and Hunter Wilson. Total number of initiates, 116; deceased members, 3.

ALPHA-KAPPA, forty-fifth chapter chartered. Established at Cornell University, Ithaca, N. Y., on May 23, 1892. Sponsors at establishment: Daniel Royse (Purdue), and Richard Johnson Putnam (Centenary). Charter members: Daniel Royse, Richard Johnson Putnam, Arthur William Herman Kaiser, James Christian Meinich Hanson, Willis Charles Ellis, Bion Lucien Burrows, Henry Curtis Earle, Charles Dunn, Harry Merrick Beach, George Warren Rulison, and Henry George Wolcott. Total number of initiates, 143; deceased members, 6.

ALPHA-LAMBDA, forty-sixth chapter chartered. Established at the University of Vermont, Burlington, Vt., on Feb. 16, 1893. Sponsors at establishment: Jeremiah Sweetser Ferguson (Maine), and Charles Prentiss Kittredge (Maine). Charter members: Tenney Hall Wheatley, Frank Nelson Guild, Bertie Duane Longe, William Stuart, John Findlay Young.

Clayton Gerald Andrews, Theodore Eli Hopkins, Leigh Hunt, Norman Brown Webber, Otis Warren Barrett, Carl Wallace Fisher, Harry DeWitt Giddings, Joseph .Benjamin Kidder, and Frederick Milo Small. Total number of initiates, 128; deceased members, 4.

ALPHA-MU, forty-seventh chapter chartered. Established at the University of North Carolina, Chapel Hill, N. C., on June 3, 1893. Sponsors at establishment: Thomas Cowper Daniels, Frank Bettis Davis, David Anderson Houston, Frank Gibbons Westbrook, Luther Thompson Hartsell, Sterling Blackwell Pierce, John William Daniels, Albert Hubbard Bangert, James Walter Wadsworth, Braxton Phifer, Samuel W. Sparger, and William Atlas Finch, all of Trinity. Charter members: George Roscoe Little, Gerard Samuel Wittson, James Spencer Lewis, Thomas Pleasant Braswell, Jr., and Thomas Menan Hooker. Total number of initiates, 33; deceased members, 1.

ALPHA-NU, forty-eighth chapter chartered. Established at Wofford College, Spartanburg, S. C., on Jan. 27, 1894. Sponsors at establishment: De La Warr Benjamin Easter (Randolph-Macon), Reginald McCreery Rawls (South Carolina), and Richard Smallwood Des Portes (South Carolina). Charter members: Benjamin Wofford Wait, Frederick Anson Cummings, John Caswell Roper, Thomas McTyeire Raysor and Nathaniel Moss Salley. Total number of initiates, 67; deceased members, 3.

ALPHA-XI, forty-ninth chapter chartered. Established at Bethel College, Russellville, Ky., on May 28, 1894. Charter withdrawn in 1902, since which time it has not been reestablished. Anti-fraternity laws do not obtain. Sponsors at establishment: Robert Alomath Cox (Southwestern Presbyterian), Thomas Maury Daniel (Southwestern Presbyterian), Matthew Gerald Lyle (Southwestern Presbyterian), Harry Wesley Borders (Southwestern Presbyterian), Lawrence Newton Byers (Southwestern Presbyterian), and others. Charter members: Holman Taylor, Alonzo Stuart Wooten, John Caldwell Browder, Howell Harrison Hopson and Julian Wilcox Courts. Total number of initiates, 45; deceased members, 3.

ALPHA-OMICRON, fiftieth chapter chartered. Established at Kentucky University, Lexington, Ky., on Sept. 7, 1894. Charter withdrawn in 1901, since which time it has not been reestablished. Anti-fraternity laws do not obtain. Sponsors at establishment: John Taylor Green (Purdue), John Van Meter Nicholas (Washington and Lee), and McKenzie Robertson Todd (Michigan). Charter members: Paul Vincent Bartlett, Michael Donoho Forman, William Wood Ballard and Morton Humphrey Bourne. Total number of initiates, 50; deceased members, 1.

ALPHA-PI, fifty-first chapter chartered. Established at Wabash College, Crawfordsville, Ind., on Feb. 1, 1895. Sponsors at establishment: Charles Brewster Randolph (Cumberland), John Taylor Green (Purdue), George Eugene Boyd (Illinois), and Birch David Coffman (Illinois). Charter members: Charles Brewster Randolph, Robert Nathaniel Todd, Felix Henry Willis, Harry Herbert McClure, and Charles Matthias Rauch. Total number of initiates, 70; deceased members, 1.

ALPHA-RHO, fifty-second chapter chartered. Established at Bowdoin College, Brunswick, Maine, on March 22, 1895. Sponsors at establishment: Charles Maurice Randlette (Maine), eleven members of Psi Chapter, and John Findlay Young, Leigh Hunt, Carl Wallace Fisher, Hugh Aaron Seager, and Ide Gill Sargeant, all of Vermont. Charter members: Clarence Edgar Baker, Ralph Wallace Crosman, Cecil Leroy Blake, Frederick Howard Dole, Joseph William Hewitt, Oscar Elmer Pease, Edwin Francis Pratt, James Edwin Rhodes, 2d, Reuel Washburn Smith, Eben Davis Lane, Ernest Charles Edwards, and Jacob Meldon Loring. Total number of initiates, 99; deceased members, 1.

ALPHA-SIGMA, fifty-third chapter chartered. Established at the Ohio State University, Columbus, Ohio, on March 22, 1895. Sponsors at establishment: William Taylor Thayer (Hampden-Sidney), John Atkinson Thayer (Swarthmore), and Frederick Neal Carr (Swarthmore). Charter members: Charles William Burkett, Renick William Dunlap, Ernest Jacob Riggs, Dora Van Buren Burkett, and Charles Franklin Sprague. Total number of initiates, 101; deceased members, 5.

ALPHA-TAU, fifty-fourth chapter chartered. Established at the Georgia School of Technology, Atlanta, Ga., on Oct. 5, 1895. Sponsors at establishment: Mark Johnston White (Mercer), George Washington Smith (Mercer), Jesse Chamblis Harris (Mercer), Lawson James Pritchard (Mercer), Henry Martin Cass (Grant), Fielding Parker Sizer (Grant), Frank Finley Hooper (Grant), and John Maynard Rutherford (Grant). Charter members: Birton Neill Wilson, James Thompson Wikle, Walter Brooks West, Charles Pinckney Rowland, Frederic Earl Solomon, Frank Barrows Freyer, Bertie William Seawell and William Barton Reynolds. Total number of initiates, 84; deceased members, 4.

ALPHA-UPSILON, fifty-fifth chapter chartered. Established at Millsaps College, Jackson, Miss., on Nov. 9, 1895. Sponsors at establishment: Thomas Bascom Holloman, Jr. (Centenary), and Joseph Fielding Robinson (Sewanee). Charter members: Charles Galloway Jones, Daniel Gilmer McLaurin, William Burwell Jones, Charles Girault Andrews, Blackshear Hamilton Locke, Henry Thompson Carley, John Holliday Holloman, Ethelbert Hines Galloway, Thomas Mitchell Lemly, and John Tillery Lewis. Total number of initiates, 109; deceased members, 0.

ALPHA-PHI, fifty-sixth chapter chartered. Established at Bucknell University, Lewisburg, Pa., on Dec. 11, 1896. Local society, Phi Epsilon, absorbed. Sponsors at establishment: James Harry Covington (Maryland Military and Naval), George Harold Powell (Cornell), and Alpha-Delta Chapter. Charter members: Merton Roscoe Collins, George Albert Jennings, Simon Ward Gilpin, Oliver John Decker, George Edward Jenkinson, Jr., William Robert Morris, Benjamin Williams Griffith, Saner Cook Bell, and Arthur Dougherty Rees. Total number of initiates, 73; deceased members, 1.

ALPHA-PSI, fifty-seventh chapter chartered. Established at the University of Nebraska, Lincoln, Neb., on Feb. 13, 1897. Sponsor at establishment: Charles Brewster Randolph (Cumberland). Charter members: Charles Alfred Turrell, Charles Frederick Schwartz, William Grant, Clarence Curtis Culver, Leonard Harman Robbins, Cassius Asa Fisher, Carl Le Roy Shuff, Le Roy Vernon Patch, and Charles Edward Matson. Total number of initiates, 104; deceased members, 1.

ALPHA-OMEGA, fifty-eighth chapter chartered. Established at William Jewell College, Liberty, Mo., on May 8, 1897. Local society, Pi Alpha Theta, absorbed. Sponsors at establishment: Charles Richardson (Emory and Henry), and William Laurence Cunningham (Washington and Lee). Charter members: John Jasper Bowman, Richard Archie· Bywaters, John Marion Word, Richard Irving Bruce, Carter Richard Bishop, Lester Carpenter Grady, and John William Sydnor. Total number of initiates, 60; deceased members, 3.

BETA-ALPHA, fifty-ninth chapter chartered. Established at Brown University, Providence, R. I., on Feb. 22, 1898. Sponsors at establishment: John Warren Davis (Bucknell), George Edward Schilling (Bucknell), Warren Robinson Austin (Vermont), Norton Royce Hotchkiss (Maryland), John Lawrence Ludwig (Virginia Polytechnic), Frank Edward Snowden (Southwestern Presbyterian), and Frederic Lee Stone (Sewanee). Charter members: Ephraim LeRoy Hart, Mellinger Edward Henry, Arthur Herbert Fitz, Charles Israel Gates, Francis Severance Johnson, William Watson Wyckoff, Luther Bentley Adams, Leonard Merrick Patton, Ernest Palmer Carr, Carlton John Patton, David Connolly Hall, and Claude Everett Stevens. Total number of initiates, 83; deceased members, 2.

BETA-BETA, sixtieth chapter chartered. Established at Richmond College, Richmond, Va, on March 5, 1898. Sponsors at establishment: Herbert Milton Martin (Randolph-Macon), Stanley Watkins Martin (Virginia Polytechnic), Lewis Fleming (Hampden-Sidney), Rives Fleming (Hampden-Sidney), James Duncan Hughlett (Randolph-Macon), Norval Thomas Hepburn (Randolph-Macon), Thomas Watson Brown (William and Mary), William Spencer Henley (William and Mary), Frank Thomas Staley (Emory and Henry) and others. Charter members: William Loftin Prince, Charles Craddock Barksdale, Robert Lee Williams, Harry Rew, William Gary Bidgood, Robert Opie Norris, Jr., Robert Nelson Pollard, and Norman Gara Woodson. Total number of initiates, 43; deceased members, c.

BETA-GAMMA, sixty-first chapter chartered, Established at the Missouri State University, Columbia, Mo., on April 6' 1898. Sponsors at establishment: George Vaughan (Arkansas), Berkeley St. John Green (Sewanee), and Abe John Myar (Arkansas). Charter members: William Henry Turner, John Crockett Edwards, Adelphus Centimus Terrell, George Gordon Robertson, Everett Pine Weatherly, David Otto Row, Judson Baker Bond, Wilford Caldwell Barnhardt, and Ernest Tate. Total number of initiates, 77; deceased members, 3.

Beta-Delta, sixty-second chapter chartered. Established at Washington and Jefferson College, Washington, Pa., on April 15, 1898. Sponsors at establishment: Rudolph Peak Lippincott (Wabash). Charter members: Rudolph Peak Lippincott, John Robert Musgrave, Homer Krepps Underwood, William Pollock Craig, Lee Dewitt Hemingway, Chas. Walter Stone, Alexander Blaikie Jobson, Earl Cubbison Cleeland, and John Charles Walter Busch. Total number of initiates, 52; deceased members, 1.

Beta-Epsilon, sixty-third chapter chartered. Established at the University of Wisconsin, Madison, Wis., on June 11, 1898. Sponsors at establishment: Mark Sands (Michigan), Guy Miltimore (Illinois), George Eugene Boyd (Illinois), Lore Alford Rogers (Maine), and Joseph Maxwell McArthur (Sewanee). Charter members: Lore Alford Rogers, Joseph Maxwell McArthur, William Brown Ford, Thomas George Nee, John Lincoln Fisher, and George Warner Mosher. Total number of initiates, 88; deceased members, 1.

Beta-Zeta, sixty-fourth chapter chartered. Established at Leland Stanford, Jr., University, Cal., on May 19, 1899. Sponsors at establishment: Frank Maytham (Cornell), and Robert Lee Stephenson (Tennessee). Charter members: Frank Maytham, Alfred Francis William Schmidt, Frederic Jewell Perry, Frank Hinman, Howard Truslow, and Roy Harry Black. Total number of initiates, 59; deceased members, 1.

Beta-Eta, sixty-fifth chapter chartered. Established at the Alabama Polytechnic Institute, Auburn, Ala., on Jan'y 20, 1900. Sponsors at establishment: Nathaniel Leslie Carpenter (Vanderbilt), James Napoleon Granade (Alabama), John Harman Taylor (Mercer), William Parker Neilson (Alabama), and Thomas Sweeney Sharp (Alabama). Charter members: Malcolm Alfred Beeson, William Forney Osborne, William Stowe Rutledge, Luther Noble Duncan, James Richard Rutland, Henry Virgil Reid, Paul Shields Haley, George Waddell Snedecor, William Lawson Thornton, and William Watson Rutland. Total number of initiates, 59; deceased members, 0.

Beta-Iota, sixty-sixth chapter chartered. Established at Lehigh University, South Bethlehem, Pa., on Nov. 28, 1900. Sponsors at establishment: the members of the Supreme Executive Committee and the delegates to the 14th Biennial Grand Conclave. Charter members: William Perry Rogers, John Stauffer Krauss, Louis Gustave Krauss, Charles Elmer Barba, Arthur Reuben Young, Henry Le Roy Fryer, Solomon W. Goldsmith, Ellis Garfield Godshalk, George Jack Walz, and John Walt Dismant. Total number of initiates, 49; deceased members, 0.

Beta-Kappa, sixty-seventh chapter chartered. Established at the New Hampshire College, Durham, N. H., on Feb. 22, 1901. Local society, Q. T. V., absorbed. Sponsors at establishment: Jeremiah Sweetser Ferguson (Maine), Charles William Burkett (Ohio State), Frederick

Symes Johnston (Ohio State), George Hoxsie Stickney (Cornell, Preston Banks Churchill (Bowdoin), Edward Trowbridge Fenley (Bowdoin), Arthur Lawrence Small (Bowdoin), Bertram Albert Warren (Brown), and William Eli Putnam (Vermont). Charter members: Irving Atwell Colby, Henry Harold Calderwood, Charles Almon Hunt, Edwin Price Jewett, Robert McArdle Keown, Elmer Eugene Lyon, Norman Allen Rollins, Edwin William Gilmartin, John Chester Kendall, Harry Moulton Lee, Abiel Abbott Livermore, William Lincoln Barker, Harry David Batchelor, Everett William Burbeck, Frank Lester Hill, Ralph Harvey Rollins, Carl Linwood Sargent, Melvin Johnson White, Percy Anderson Campbell, Frank Lurling Hadley, Thomas Jefferson Laton, Levi Joseph Marsh, Joseph French Blodgett, and Charles Emery Robertson. Total number of initiates, 90; deceased members, 0.

BETA-LAMBDA, sixty-eighth chapter chartered. Established at the University of Georgia, Athens, Ga., on March 16, 1901. Sponsors at establishment: Israel Mercer Putnam (Vanderbilt), Robert Clinton Stephens (Mercer), Bradford Enoch Roughton, Jr. (Mercer), Joseph Albert Hall, Jr., John Gillespie Johnson, Milton Graham Smith, Paul Howes Norcross, Hugh O'Keefe Kendrick, Samuel Warren Mays and Luther Love Hunnicutt, all of Georgia Tech. Charter members: Israel Mercer Putnam, Charles Johns Moore, Marvin McDonald Dickinson, John Earle Overby McCalla, Marion Stinson Monk, John Christian Koch, Oscar John Coogler, George Washington Threlkeld, Walter Barnett Shaw, and Paul Jones King. Total number of initiates, 38; deceased members, 0.

BETA-MU, sixty-ninth chapter chartered. Established at the University of Minnesota, Minneapolis, Minn., on April 6, 1901. Local society Alpha Theta absorbed. Sponsors at establishment: Walter Wallace Tyler (Vermont), William Robt. Morris (Bucknell), Rufus Milton Barnes (Pennsylvania), Mervin Eber Alcott (Lake Forest), Clarence Eugene Abbott (Wisconsin), John Morledge Woy (Wisconsin) and James Russell Hobbins (Wisconsin). Charter members: Edward Alford Ecklund, Charles Parker Sterling, George Francis Shea, Frank Charles Hughes, Emory Lee Jewell, Lyman Joseph Howes, Morton Lewis McBride, Samuel Doak Lowery, William Henry Shea, Jr., and Adrian Daniel Mastenbrook. Total number of initiates, 61; deceased members, 1.

BETA-NU, seventieth chapter chartered. Established at the Kentucky State College, Lexington, Ky., on April 5, 1901. Sponsors at establishment: William Wood Ballard (Kentucky), James Aylmer Slack (Bethel), Benjamin Talbott Hume, Jr. (Kentucky), Waller Pendleton Eubank (Bethel), Madison Ashby Hart (Kentucky), Dawson Chambers (Kentucky), and others. Charter members: Lewis Andrew Darling, James Aylmer Slack, Benjamin Talbott Hume, Jr., John Henry Leon Vogt, Waller Pendleton Eubank, John Edwin Brown, George William Headley, Jr., Butler Fauntleroy Thompson, Charles Leon Peckinpaugh, Samuel Fletcher Parker, Charles Wright Atkinson, and Herman Frederick Scholtz. Total number of initiates, 40; deceased members, 1.

BETA-XI, seventy-first chapter chartered. Established at the University of California, Berkeley, Cal., on Aug. 24, 1901. Local society Beta Kappa Delta absorbed. Sponsors at establishment: Frederick Jewell Perry (Stanford), Edward Marion Walsh (Michigan), Elmer Guy Ryker (Michigan), Peter James Crosby (Michigan), Thomas Stanley Evans (George Washington), William Henry Beard (George Washington), Carl Wallace Fisher (Vermont), Robert Lee Stephenson (Tennessee), Roy Harry Black (Stanford), Alfred Francis William Schmidt (Stanford), Ernest Stoddard Page (Stanford), Clarence Winslow Page (Stanford), Claude Bailey Gillespie (Stanford), Frank Hinman (Stanford), Harry Clifford Lucas (Stanford), and Nathan Gardiner Symonds (Stanford). Charter members: Lawrence Stephen O'Toole, Boutwell Dunlap, Clarence Casebolt Dakin, Frederick Holroyd Dakin, Jr., Charles Thomason Dozier, Christopher Hatton Aspland, William Whitehead Hurlburt, and Robert Weitbrec Cooper. Total number of initiates, 48; deceased members, 0.

BETA-OMICRON, seventy-second chapter chartered. Established at Denver University, Denver, Col., on Feb. 8, 1902. Sponsors at establishment: John Randolph Neal (Tennessee), Edmond Plumb Boynton (Cornell), Franklin Houston Morrison (Ohio), and William Marshall Robinson (Wm. Jewell). Charter members: Davis McArthur Carson, Justin Hiram Haynes, William Angus Mitchell, William James Perkins. Charles Frederick Morris, Frank Leslie Veatch, and Samuel Clifford Carnes. Total number of initiates, 40; deceased members, 1.

BETA-PI, seventy-third chapter chartered. Established at Dickinson College, Carlisle, Pa., on Feb. 7, 1902. Local society, Pi Gamma Alpha. absorbed. Sponsors at establishment: John Warren Davis (Bucknell), Frank Jones Kier (Pennsylvania), Lewis Bayard Custer (Bucknell), Carroll Caruthers (Bucknell), David Robinson Walkinshaw (Bucknell), Walter Wetmore Senn (Bucknell), Charles Arthur Woodard (Bucknell), Joseph Earl Hill (Lehigh), Henry LeRoy Fryer (Lehigh), John Rockev Decker (Pennsylvania State), Edward Nathan Zern (Pennsylvania State), James Vance Kyle (Pennsylvania State). George Edgar Diehl (Pennsylvania State), Robert Wallace Wray (Pennsylvania State). James Ellis Harvey (Pennsylvania State), and William Van Gundia Detwiler (Pennsylvania State). Charter members: Frank Thompson Bell, Ulysses Simpson Wright, William Edward Myers, Agis Aldridge McCrone, Robert Clarence Peters, Curvin Henry Gingrich, Thomas Edwin Redding. John Wycliffe Yost, Charles Wesley Taylor, Louis Crawford Carroll, and Herbert Jerrel Belting. Total number of initiates, 45; deceased members, 0.

BETA-RHO, seventy-fourth chapter chartered. Established at the State University of Iowa, Iowa City, Iowa, on Sep. 27, 1902. Local society Phi Upsilon absorbed. Sponsors at establishment: Mark Sands (Michigan), Samuel Berkley Sloan (Nebraska), William Karl Herrick (Lake Forest), and Adrian Daniel Mastenbrook (Minnesota). Charter members:

Frederick Henry Luhman, Edwin Calhoun Arthur, John Augustus Mc-
Kenzie, Thomas Corwin Smith, John Paul Redmond, Francis Nugent,
Harvey Le Roy Dye, Harold Beecher Strong, Walter Lynn Du Bois,
Willard Carlisle Swigart, Bert Blaine Burnquist, and Thomas Cyrus
Doran. Total number of initiates, 58; deceased members, o.

BETA-SIGMA, seventy-fifth chapter chartered. Established at Washington University, St. Louis, Mo., on Nov. 22, 1902. Sponsors at estab-
ishment: Charles Richardson (Emory and Henry), William Brownlow Latta (Arkansas), Harvey Field Parker (Missouri), Edwin Dwight Smith
(Missouri), Malcolm Phelps Post (Ohio State), Oliver Thul Johnson
(Missouri), Hugh Beverly Hill (Arkansas), Thomas Robertson Hill (Ar-
kansas), William Hendry Prentice, Jr. (Purdue),Thos. Hendricks David
(Purdue), Royal Lee Bunch (William Jewell), Carter Richard Bishop
(William Jewell), Bartlett Roper Bishop (William Jewell), Walter Frank
Koken (Missouri), John Henry Rogers, Jr. (Purdue), Roscoe Florence An-
derson (Missouri), Patrick Henry Aylett (William and Mary), William
Smith Warner (Wisconsin), Rockwell Smith Brank (Virginia) and Rich-
ard Thomas Brownrigg (Sewanee). Charter members: William Brownlow
Latta, Harry Field Parker, Robert Funkhouser, Sargent F. Jones, David
Carson Goodman, and Oscar Kilby. Total number of initiates, 32; de-
ceased members, I.

BETA-TAU, seventy-sixth chapter chartered. Established at Baker
University, Baldwin, Kans., on Feb. 2, 1903. Local society, "Skull and
Bones," absorbed. Sponsors at establishment: Charles Richardson (Emory
and Henry), and Denny Coulter Simrall, Hume Stanley White, Esty
Angus Julian, Madison Smith Slaughter, Lewis Wilbur Cohen, Ray-
mond Prewitt Estil, and John Frank Guyton, all of William Jewell.
Charter members: Arthur Roy Bowman, Walter Hodgin Case, Alpha
Mills Ebright, Rollo Wood Coleman, Charles Everett Ely, Edwin Adam
Britsch, Jesse Cecil Denious, Burr Howey Ozment, Don Earl Waggoner,
Wm. Wesley Rubel, Henry Farrar Durkee, Jesse Howard Moore, Arden
Heman Douglass, and Samuel Everett Urner. Total number of initi-
ates, 49; deceased members, o.

BETA-UPSILON, seventy-seventh chapter chartered. Established at the
North Carolina College of Agriculture and Mechanic Arts, Raleigh,
N. C., on Feb. 23, 1903. Sponsors at establishment: Herbert Milton
Martin (Randolph-Macon), Charles William Burkett (Ohio State),
Daniel Price Withers (Virginia), Albert Fuller Patton (Hampden-
Sidney), Hugh O'Keefe Kendrick (Georgia Tech.), John Chester
Kendall (New Hampshire), Daniel Shuford Murph (Wofford), Der-
mot Shemwell (Davidson), Thomas Walter Smith, Jr. (Trinity),
Lemuel Hardy Gibbons (Trinity), Wilson Grinter Puryear (Trinity),
Robert Anderson Brown (Trinity), Charles Gibbons (Trinity), Lloyd
Kirby Wooten (Trinity), William Archer Brown (Trinity), Charles
Thomas Woollen (North Carolina), Lawrence Archdale Tomlinson (Trin-

ity), and William Lawrence Grimes (North Carolina). Charter members:
Leslie Norwood Boney, Charles Leicester Creech, Eugene English Cul-
breth, Walter Lee Darden, Edward Hayes Ricks, Jarvis Benjamin Hard-
ing, Branton Faison Huggins, William Richardson, Jr., William Miller
Chambers, Frederic Watson Hadley, George Green Lynch, Jr., Charles
Wigg Martin, James Hicks Pierce, Edward Griffith Porter, Jr., Charles
Tennent Venable, and Lewis Taylor Winston. Total number of initi-
ates, 42; deceased members, 0.

BETA-PHI, seventy-eighth chapter chartered. Established at Case
School of Applied Science, Cleveland, O., on Nov. 26, 1903. Local so-
ciety, Phi Alpha Chi, absorbed. Sponsors at establishment: Mark Sands
(Michigan), George Locke Crosby (Millsaps), Dwight Spencer Anderson
(Ohio State University), Edward Bovey Armbruster (Ohio State),
Sherman Bronson Randall (Ohio State), William Benson Wal-
ling (Stanford), James Leonard Moore (Arkansas), Nathaniel Gardi-
ner Symonds (Stanford), Victor Emile Thebaud (Cornell), and Her-
bert Coward (Cornell). Charter members: Rudolph Armandos Droege,
Arthur Edwin Schaefer, Raymond Bertram Perry, Irving Fink Laucks,
Egbert Richard Morrison, Hallie Summerville Hall, Paul Payson Elliott,
Myrl John Falkenburg, Orrie John Mills, Herbert Harlow Freese, and
Alvah Meade Clark. Total number of initiates, 41; deceased members, 0.

BETA-CHI, seventy-ninth chapter chartered. Established at the Missouri School of Mines, Rolla, Mo., on Dec. 19, 1903. Sponsors at establishment; Charles Richardson (Emory and Henry), Denny Coulter Simrall (William Jewell), Flippin Martin Cook (Arkansas), Clifton Langs-
dale (Missouri), Oliver Thul Johnson (Missouri), and Esty Angus Julian
(William Jewell). Charter members: John Severin Schroeder, Jr., Leslie Burson Emry, Matthew Vincent Quinn, Charles Le Clair King, Orsi
Paul Allee, George Horton Blackman, Henry Hartzell, Jr., David Choplin Evans, Dale Coleman Barnard, and Walter White McMillen. Total
number of initiates, 29; deceased members, 0.

BETA-PSI, eightieth chapter chartered. Established at the University
of Washington, Seattle, Wash., on Dec. 15, 1903. Sponsors at establishment: Frederic Jewell Perry (Stanford), William Robert Bell (Maryland Military and Naval), and Roy Overman Hadley (Stanford). Charter members: Winford Lee Lewis, John Charles Rathbun, Arthur Roy
Terpening, Frank Vedder Taylor, and John Ruskin Slattery. Total
number of initiates, 32; deceased members, 0.

BETA-OMEGA, eighty-first chapter chartered. Established at Colorado
College, Colorado Springs, Colo., on March 12, 1904; Local society Phi
Upsilon Sigma absorbed. Sponsors at establishment: John Randolph Neal
(Tennessee), Justin Hiram Haynes (Denver), St. George Tucker (Wil-
liam and Mary), George Warner Mosher (Wisconsin), William Edward
Foley (Denver), Charles Frederick Morris (Denver), Davis McArthur
Carson (Denver), Robert Morrison Drysdale (Denver), George Berkeley

Holderer (Denver), and Frank Leslie Veatch (Denver). Charter members: James McClure Platt, George Gardner, Jr., William John Wallrich, Elliot Eugene Reyer, Augustus Du Bois Forbush, Charles School Leuchtenburg, Philip Fitch, Walter Christopher Tegtmeyer, and Albert Cobert. Total number of initiates, 28; deceased members, o.

GAMMA-ALPHA, eighty-second chapter chartered. Established at the University of Oregon, Eugene, Ore., on April 16, 1904. Sponsors at establishment: Frederic Jewell Perry (Stanford), and Schiller Brents Hermann (Washington and Lee). Charter members: Walter Lincoln Whittlesey, John Frederick Staver, Charles Lois Campbell, David Graham, Vernor Wayne Tomlinson, Chester Wesley Washburne, Ivan Edward Oakes, Cloan Norris Perkins, James Franklin Donnelly, Chester Harvard Starr, John Randolph Latourette, Harry Logan Raffety, Harley Glafke, Gordon Chamberlain Moores and John Currin Veatch. Total number of initiates, 28; deceased members, o.

GAMMA-BETA, eighty-third chapter chartered. Established at the University of Chicago, Chicago, Ill., on May 11, 1904. Local society "The Bronze Shield" absorbed. Sponsors at establishment: Mark Sands (Michigan), Robert Allen Lackey (Purdue), Jesse Elmer Roberts (Michigan), Edwin Calhoun Arthur (Iowa), Robert Franklin Carr, Jr. (Illinois), Augustus Ruffner (West Virginia), Walter Scott Carr (Illinois), Chas. Chandler (Swarthmore), Frank Howe Cornell (Illinois); and others. Charter members: Samuel Crawford Ross, James Roy Ozanne, Lyford Paterson Edwards, Edward Lyman Cornell, Henry Winford Bigelow, Jr., John Frederick Tobin, Paul Temple Ramsey, Bernard Iddings Bell, and Edward Grattan Ince. Total number of initiates, 26; deceased members, o.

GAMMA-GAMMA, eighty-fourth chapter chartered. Established at the Colorado School of Mines, Golden, Col., on May 21, 1904. Sponsors at establishment: John Randolph Neal (Tennessee), Wilbur Franklin Denious (Denver), John Morledge Woy (Wisconsin), Scott Watson (Millsaps), Davis McArthur Carson (Denver), James Rumney Killian (Texas), Frederic Richter Wright (Denver), Clarence Atkins Ward (Denver), William Edward Foley (Denver), Frank Leslie Veatch (Denver), Charles Frederic Morris (Denver), George Berkeley Holderer (Denver), and others. Charter members: Davis MacArthur Carson, Scott Watson, John Jerome Cory, Joseph Francis O'Byrne, Ernest Frederick Stoeckley, Edward Merewether, Ralph Wyatt Shumway, and Maynard James Trott. Total number of initiates, 29; deceased members, o.

GAMMA-DELTA, eighty-fifth chapter chartered. Established at the Massachusetts State College, Amherst, Mass., on June 13, 1904. Local society D. G. K., absorbed. Sponsors at establishment: Jeremiah Sweetser Ferguson (Maine), Frank Stevens Tolman (Maine), Lincoln Ross Colcord (Maine), George Hoxsie Stickney (Cornell), Jesse Leonti Bliss (Cornell), Charles Austin Coburn (Vermont), Irwin Spear (Vermont,

Norris W. Chapman (Vermont), Harley W. Heath (Vermont), and Neill Starr Franklin (New Hampshire). Charter members: Clifford Franklin Elwood, Reuben Raymond Raymoth, John Franklin Lyman, Bertram Tupper, James Richard Kelton, Charles Sheldon Holcomb, Harold Foss Tompson, Edward Thorndike Ladd, Percy Frederic Williams, Alexander Henry Moore, Everett Pike Mudge, Herman Augustus Suhlke, Stanley Sawyer Rogers, Edwin Hobart Scott, Charles Walter Carpenter, Arthur Huguenin Armstrong, Arthur William Higgins, George Franklin Smith, Calder Sankey Stoddard, George Augustus Dearth, Joseph Otis Chapman, and Harold Edward Alley. Total number of initiatese, 101; deceased members, 1.

GAMMA-EPSILON, eighty-sixth chapter chartered. Established at Dartmouth College, Hanover, N. H., on April 11, 1905. Local society Beta Gamma absorbed. Sponsors at establishment: Jeremiah Sweetser Ferguson (Maine), Homer Francis Brown (Maine), and others. Charter members: Frederick Warren Jenkins, Albion Keith Spofford, Carl Folsom Getchell, Homer Francis Brown, Harry Allen McMore, Joseph Augustine O'Connor, Floyd Tangier Smith, Jerome Ambrose McDonald, and Walter Goble Wehrle. Total number of initiates, 32; deceased members, 0.

GAMMA-ZETA, eighty-seventh chapter chartered. Established at New York University, New York, N. Y., on April 6, 1905. Sponsors at establishment: Jeremiah Sweetser Ferguson (Maine), Guy Thomas Viskniskki (Swarthmore), Frederic Lee Stone (Sewanee), William Labaree Flye (Bowdoin), John Taylor Green (Purdue), Louis Warner Riggs (Maine), Sidney Rawson Perry (Washington and Lee), Samuel Bell Thomas (Southwestern), James Bryson McKeage (Southwestern Presbyterian), Abner McGehee, Jr. (Arkansas), William Watson Wyckoff (Brown), Byron Albert Kilbourne (Cornell), and others. Charter members: Richard Joshua Brown, George William Bartelmez, Willis Brooks Davis, Alfred Starr Griffiths, Charles McAvoy, Edwin McQueen, Adrian Charles Griffin, George Scudder Jervis, and Christian Henry Von Bargen. Total number of initiates, 15; deceased members, 0.

GAMMA-ETA, eighty-eighth chapter chartered. Established at Harvard University, Cambridge, Mass., on June 24, 1905. Local society Pi Upsilon absorbed. Sponsors at establishment: Stanley Watkins Martin (Virginia Polytechnic), Jeremiah Sweetser Ferguson (Maine), George Hoxsie Stickney (Cornell), Joseph Sterry Lamson (California), Samuel Townsend Stewart (Swarthmore), James Thompson McDonald (Washington and Jefferson), Robert Emmett Craig (Southwestern Presbyterian), members of the Boston Alumni Chapter, and representatives from the New England Chapters. Charter members: Charles Luther Olds, Jr., Norman Devereux Olds, James Thayer Fenner, Arthur Pray Rice, Lyman Calvin Goodrich, Robert Carver Diserens, Philip Wescott Lawrence Cox, Lawrence Burns Webster, Arthur Evans Wood, Ralph William Smiley, Henry Odin Tilton, George Edwin Eversole, Raymond

John Scully, Harries Arthur Mumma, Clifford Warren Maish, ·and Arthur Edwin Van Bibber. Total number of initiates, 29; deceased members, 0.

GAMMA-THETA, eighty-ninth chapter chartered. Established at the University of Idaho, Moscow, Id., on Sep. 30, 1905. Local society Sigma Delta Alpha absorbed. Sponsors at establishment: Frederic Jewell Perry (Stanford), Frederick Joseph Carver (Nebraska), Philip Tindall (George Washington), William Kelly Roosevelt (Stanford), Brice Loveland Trost (Stanford), and Verne Cecil Hurlbut (Stanford). Charter members: Roy Wethered, Floyd Dwight Angel, James William Galloway, Victor Emanuel Price, Nicholas Collins Sheridan, Louis James Fogle, William Madison Snow, Harry Baxter Noble, C. C. Gee, George Herbert Wyman, Jr., William Wilson Goble, Thomas Dunlap Matthews, Thomas Estil Hunter, William Enderle Robertson, Wilfred Adamson. William Nelson Thomas, Harry T. Hunter, and John Francis Carson. Total number of initiates, 29; deceased members, 0.

GAMMA-IOTA, ninetieth chapter chartered. Established at Syracuse University, Syracuse, N. Y., on May 15, 1906. Sponsors at establishment: Jeremiah Sweetser Ferguson (Maine), Almon Andrus Jaynes (Brown), Claude Burton Dakin (Brown), Willard Albertson Rill (George Washington), Reenen Jacob Van Reenen (Lehigh), Samuel Henry Salisbury, Jr. (Lehigh), Edwin McQueen (New York), and Austin Wright Eddy (New York). Charter members: Garrett Putnam Serviss Cross, Frederick Joseph Shepherd, Daniel Henry Brooks, William Ross Van Housen, Granville Avery Waters, William Francis Evans, Charles Eugene De Long, Walter F. Shaw, Charles Stuart Knight, Walter Rollo Hibbard, and Ebenezer Merritt Larkin. Total number of initiates, 18; deceased members, 0.

GAMMA-KAPPA, ninety-first chapter chartered. Established at the University of Oklahoma, Norman, Okla., on June 7, 1906. Local society Alpha Delta Sigma absorbed. Sponsors at establishment: David Connolly Hall (Brown), George Carl Abernathy (Arkansas), Theodore Plumber Bringhurst (Southwestern Presbyterian), Clarence Charles Buxton (William Jewell), Charles Ulrich Connellee (Arkansas), and Thomas Finley Munday (Bethel). Charter members: Homer Charles Washburn, William Hancock Low, Charles Daniel Johnson, Arthur Maxwell Alden, Arthur Roberts Swank, William Gladstone Lemmon, Ralph Harold Dangerfield, Walter Lee Ransom, Earl Tobias Miller, Frederick Leroy Allen, Frederick Marion Trotter, Clarence Alexander Ambrister, and George Lawrie Kellar. Total number of initiates, 12; deceased members, 0.

CPSIA information can be obtained
at www.ICGtesting.com
Printed in the USA
LVHW031817181218
600899LV00003B/390/P

9 781333 592325